ASSOCIATION 4.0™

AN ENTREPRENEURIAL APPROACH TO RISK, COURAGE, AND TRANSFORMATION

Cover designed by .orgCompanies, LLC

Visit our website at www.positioningforsuccessbook.com

Printed in the United States of America

First Printing: February 2020
Amazon

ISBN: 9781660111718

CONTENTS

FOREWORD

This book tells the stories of how some of the best leaders in the association industry navigate their businesses through disruption and change.

Over the last 30 years, I have been employed by an association management company, two stand-alone associations, and three consultancies. I have been involved with organizations that are household names and others that, even in a burst of creativity, you might not imagine exist.

Helping those diverse groups develop business strategies that translate vision into action is a significant focus of mine. One of the ironies of this work is that associations sometimes behave so differently than the industries they represent. While the marketplace focuses on the future, associations wear their history and tradition as a badge of honor. In the midst of a business world driven by invention, innovation, and profit, associations revolve around traditional interpretations of mission and service.

That more passive approach worked well in a slower environment. But it doesn't serve associations or their members when matched against a technological revolution that is re-creating or destroying business and professions with ease. It's time for bolder strategies.

That's why this book is important. Business owners who serve the association community start from scratch and come through their own ranks. One minute they're the CEO describing their vision to a customer, and the next they might be the receptionist fielding calls. It takes courage, ingenuity, and the willingness to learn and adapt to grow a business from the ground up. These are the same qualities that are needed to remain relevant when the idea of relevance is in constant flux. Association CEOs can learn a lot from these extraordinary supplier partners.

This book does not provide step-by-step recipes or a mold to reshape your business model. But you will find plenty of real-life examples of how creativity, persistence, and trial and error helped these entrepreneurs survive difficult situations, thrive, and change the disruptions they faced into opportunity.

Making the space for creativity to grow is a recurring theme. As a management consultant, I learned a long time ago that in order to introduce innovation, it's helpful to break it down in terms of the significance for people, processes, and technology. Every chapter of this book illustrates a different perspective on how to accomplish that goal. The questions at the end of each interview provide an opportunity to discuss and explore how your organization might abandon outdated initiatives, discover new energy, motivate teams, and position itself for success.

This is a fascinating era in business. People around the globe can collaborate on projects. Virtual teams are on the rise, and they are the future of work. To effectively use the fantastic technology at our disposal we need to create cultures of acceptance and adaptation. We must be ready and willing to become transformers. As you meet the entrepreneurs in this book and discover their stories, you'll come to understand that to survive, organizations must continue to reinvent themselves. Transformation is not a single event; it is an endless process.

By Sharon Rice, Managing Director Business Strategy, .orgSource.

INTRODUCTION

Meet the Transformers

The transformers love solving the thorny problems that cause the rest of us to tear our hair out. They welcome disruption and use it to grow business. They change color as easily as chameleons and confront risk with the cool of derivatives traders. If you are an association leader or anyone who wants to thrive in a new business environment, the transformers are people that you need to meet.

This book includes interviews with twenty-four entrepreneurs whom we consider to be transformers. They have learned to push forward, even when the ground is shifting under their feet. Their stories are funny, motivational, sometimes a little sad, and always inspiring. Above all, these interviews are filled with advice about how to successfully navigate Association 4.0™.

Acknowledge Danger/Seize Opportunity

You've probably heard John F. Kennedy's famous quote about the dual nature of crisis. "In a crisis, be aware of the danger—but recognize the opportunity." That concept has special relevance for the association industry at this moment in time. We are at a crossroads. The possibility exists for both extinction and growth. To keep up with the speed of business and technology, associations are called on to act in ways that will make them uncomfortable. They will need to move away from preservation and conservation and toward transformation. But for organizations that are risk averse, steeped in layers of bureaucracy or strapped with outdated business models, the environment can seem precarious.

Five years ago, we realized that major shifts in our industry were on the horizon. We began asking leaders in our network and our customer base to consider how associations must change not only what they do, but who they are in order to stay relevant. We talked to more than 200 association leaders and vendor partners from across the world. As a result of what we learned from those conversations, we took several significant steps. We established .orgCommunity, a membership organization for forward-thinking leaders. We grew .orgSource, our consulting business, into .orgCompanies and leveraged our technological expertise to include a 360-degree approach to strategy in the age of digital transformation. Last but not least, we wrote our first book, *Association 4.0—Positioning for Success in an Era of Disruption.*

Experiment, Innovate, Adapt

The writing of that book was motivated by a desire to learn more about how some of the most innovative leaders in the association arena are preparing for what we call Association 4.0, or the impact that a new industrial revolution will make on our community.

> *The fourth industrial revolution is happening now. It is essentially the convergence of the physical, biological and virtual worlds. We are experiencing the next industrial revolution characterized by advanced technologies such as artificial intelligence, machine learning, 3D printing, robotics, autonomous vehicles, sensors, cloud computing and software as service. Because of artificial intelligence, devices make their own decisions, connecting people to*

> *both technology and other people in ways not even yet imagined today. The fourth industrial revolution signifies a new age for all industries. Association 4.0 is the name we've chosen to identify the leap our profession is about to make and needs to make.*

The internet has precipitated the most significant cultural renaissance since the printing press, and it is only at the beginning of its technological lifetime—just twenty years old. This fourth industrial revolution is powered by digital innovations that are coming to maturity and transforming business, workers, and the workplace in a way that no other inventions have done before. The environment is fraught with emergent challenges: competitors reinventing traditional business models; changing demographic, regulatory, and sociopolitical conditions; new modes of work; and an ongoing paradigm shift in how individuals communicate with one another and engage with organizations.

In researching our first book, we discovered that the most successful association CEOs are adopting a unique approach to this changing landscape. They are finding ways to experiment and mitigate risk, developing hubs of innovation within their organizations and using the latest technology to gain a deep understanding about their members' needs. Some leaders are even restructuring their governance to accommodate a responsive and nimble business strategy.

In other words, these CEOs are acting like transformers. As dyed-in-the-wool entrepreneurs ourselves, we wanted to explore this interesting phenomenon more thoroughly. So we set out to interview the most entrepreneurial people in our community. Many of them are leaders of partner businesses, but several are also association executives.

We asked questions about their personal career journeys—where they find passion and inspiration and how they manage and grow their companies. These leaders, like a close family friend, are in the unique position of knowing about the skeletons in the association closet. But they are also removed enough from the relationship to see the dynamics from a more objective perspective. We wanted to hear their thoughts about the future of this industry and learn how they believe associations must adapt in order to thrive.

With every entrepreneur we interviewed, we became more convinced that Association 4.0 is going to require associations to behave more like start-ups and leaders to function more like entrepreneurs. Although all our contributors saw the landscape through a different lens, many common themes emerged. Here's a small sample of the observations and advice you'll discover in the pages that follow:

"Association executives have to see their entire ecosystem. They need to look beyond the tight-knit industry definition of the profession they represent to the bigger picture. Based on our research and experience, that more global perspective starts at the top. The digital age is all about leadership. It's the style of the CEO and executive team that drives the governance and the culture." **Don Dea and Hugh Lee, Co-Founders, Fusion Productions**

"The phone in your pocket has 100,000 times more power than the processor that landed the moon rover. Everything has changed. When I started with the firm, our product was a cross-platforming tool. At the time that model was valid. When it became obsolete, we moved on to the next problem. We reviewed our clients' needs and studied their bleeding points to discover how we could build on our strengths and continue to serve. It's a process of evaluation and evolution. Success isn't just a matter of whether people need your product, it extends to how you deliver, price, and support what you sell." **Joseph Knecht, CEO, Managing Director, Proteus.co**

"Coupling innovation and associations creates an interesting dichotomy. People think of entrepreneurship as fast. We talk about failing fast and learning from failure. I agree with that approach in a small business, but larger organizations need to be patient with the cyclical process. This can be challenging for board members. It's difficult to have enthusiasm for initiatives that may not begin or end on their watch. The board must understand that a big project, like HFMA's Netflix of Associations, includes many smaller entrepreneurial and operational initiatives. True innovation—the strategies that breathe growth and energy into an organization, require perseverance and a commitment to ongoing evolution." **Garth Jordan, Senior Vice President, Corporate Strategy, Healthcare Financial Management Association**

"One of the things that we measure in our cultural assessments is how good organizations are at getting an outside perspective on what is happening internally. What people want today is old news. The trick is to determine what customers will ask for next. Being entrepreneurial means predicting people's needs twelve months or three or even five years from now." **Charlie Judy, Founder, WorkXO.**

Become a Transformer

Every week we receive calls from executives who are concerned about their association's future. We are asked for help with:

- Capturing the attention of a younger generation
- Boosting declining event registration
- Growing and engaging membership
- Identifying new sources of revenue
- Maximizing social media and adapting content

Although this book is not intended to be a "how to" or a blueprint, you'll find multiple recommendations for each of these challenges. We hope you'll think of the interviews like a dialogue with a group of trusted colleagues. Each chapter concludes with questions designed to provoke discussion about how your organization is tackling related issues. Our contributors were happy to share their professional journeys. Their failure, success, and advice is offered in the hope that those experiences will help you and your organization become transformers—innovative and inspired leaders who will build the culture needed to thrive in Industry 4.0 and beyond.

CHAPTER 1: BUDZIAK AND ORDONEZ

TO GROW A BUSINESS, BE PREPARED TO GROW YOURSELF

Sherry Budziak and Kevin Ordonez,

Co-Founders, .orgCompanies

"Vision without action is merely a dream. Action without vision just passes the time. Vision with action can change the world."—Joel A. Barker

A compelling vision guides Sherry Budziak and Kevin Ordonez in both their professional and personal lives. Their consultancy, .orgSource, has been a leader in inventing the future for associations and positioning them for success since 2005. Both Budziak and Ordonez discovered that inspiration early in their careers.

"My work is my vocation, my passion, and the realization of a childhood dream; I've wanted to be a nonprofit professional for almost as long as I can remember," says Budziak. "I am also a dyed-in-the-wool entrepreneur. These two, sometimes divergent interests, have found a happy marriage in my consulting company .orgSource and in .orgCompanies, our more recent, and deeper dive, into supporting association leaders.

"The association space gives me the opportunity to exercise skills that come naturally, such as resolving complex problems, identifying challenges and opportunities, and launching new ventures. It's also where I've learned to approach the unknown with enthusiasm and to embrace being an innovator and an agent of change."

Ordonez shared that same early passion. "Since the day I first stuck a toe into the workplace, I've taken these words from Steve Jobs seriously. Jobs said, 'The people who are crazy enough to think that they can change the world, are the ones who do.' I strive to live, breathe, and think like an entrepreneur and to bring that level of commitment to my work in the association community. I've been riding the cutting edge of technology and loving it for as long as I can remember. .orgCommunity is the sixth company that I have helped grow from the ground up. My dream of being a software/technology entrepreneur has a perfect home in the association space.

"Having a powerful vision has guided my journey and helped me get through all the different twists and turns," Ordonez notes. "It is a buffer against the negativity and misunderstanding that a new business owner inevitably encounters. Vision gives you the courage to keep your eye on the ball and the enthusiasm to take others along with you on the journey. My very first sales presentation was a lesson in the importance of vision. I'd been up all night preparing. In a perfect example of Murphy's Law, while I was finalizing the demo system on the plane, my laptop crashed. All I had left was a handful of screen shots of the system that I had printed. My belief in the product was strong enough to close that deal without any other bells and whistles."

Budziak agrees. "As an entrepreneur, you need the ability to identify a challenge and create a business that can solve that problem." But she adds, "You must also have the capacity to bring your vision to life and the stomach to tolerate the risk involved."

Put Untapped Talent to Work

Budziak was fortunate that her early entrepreneurial experiences did not include the financial trial by fire that many new business owners face. "My first association job was in the Communications Department at the American Association of Neurological Surgeons," she recalls. "I'm not sure what I expected, but I wasn't involved in lofty activities such as managing disaster relief or feeding the homeless. I was typing, filing, and writing an occasional, barely newsworthy press release. A glimmer of hope came when the #2 at AANS, David Martin, CAE (who also contributed to the book Association 4.0 – Positioning for Success in an Era of Disruption) made me an offer I couldn't refuse. He proposed that I worked with a team to build the association's first website which was, actually, the first ever website for an association. I wasn't sure exactly what I had signed up for. But it sounded exciting. After work I went straight to Barnes and Noble and bought as many books on HTML as my paycheck would allow.

"My budding career in the brave new tech world ended when politics dissolved the umbrella organization I'd been working under, and, like Dorothy, I landed back in Kansas (the Communications Department). However, there weren't many association people building websites at the time, and word about my skills was running through the grapevine. The American Academy of

Dermatology made me an offer that promised to deliver on a couple of the things I enjoy most—solving problems and being an innovator. They wanted me to start a for-profit subsidiary to develop websites for other organizations. To sweeten the deal, I was told that if the project wasn't successful, I'd be given a job somewhere else in the association. It was a great launch for a new entrepreneur. I was able to discover the thrill of building something from the ground up without any financial investment or real personal risk."

Those early career experiences shaped Budziak's approach to business as well as her views on cultivating creativity and invention. "Although I was protected by the infrastructure of an association, there were many unknowns," she says. "During my first sales presentation to a medical association, when the board president asked me how much our website proposal would cost, I looked at the neophyte programmer I'd just hired. After waiting a beat, during which the programmer was silent, I said $5,000. The board approved the offer. It probably cost $50,000 of staff time to build that site, but I learned quickly to be comfortable with the unknown."

Budziak sees the opportunities she was given as an example that other association leaders could follow. "The executive director nor the board were concerned about the possibility that I might fail. Taking a chance on me wasn't a significant financial risk weighed against the possible returns. They were willing to trust me to make good decisions and grow the business. That faith paid off. Over the next nine years our company, NetOn-line, successfully served more than 150 organizations with website development and maintenance.

"Giving innovation room to grow is something I'm passionate about, and it's one of the significant lessons in this book. Every organization has this resource—people like my younger self with the itch to experiment, build, and solve problems. Kevin and I encounter untapped talent on a regular basis. These are people who, if given the chance to innovate, could really help their organizations shine."

Make a Habit of Evolution

Budziak and Ordonez share the restless spirit that refuses to allow them to stand still. Both constantly look up the ladder to the next rung. As early promoters of technology to the association community, their paths crossed frequently. Ordonez's association management system (AMS) product and Budziak's digital strategy strengths were a natural affiliation, and eventually, the two began sharing resources and coordinating product demonstrations.

As Budziak grew a network of information technology (IT) entrepreneurs, she began to consider the possibility of becoming a business owner herself. People, especially her family, questioned why she would want to abandon a great job with a steady paycheck for an unknown future. But Budziak was convinced that she needed to follow her vision even though she had yet to discover exactly where it would lead.

"To clarify my goals, I made a list of the things that I love to do and the things that I would only do if I were starving," says Budziak. "It turned out that there weren't many full-time jobs that included all the activities that made my top ten. That reality provided the motivation to start my own consulting business. Because I had been running a web development company for nine years, people expected me to focus in that area. But having taken a hard look at myself, I knew that scope would be too narrow. Problem-solving had come out as the first place where I want to spend my time, so I decided to build my business around that core skill. I guess I solved my own problem by starting a company to do what I love, which is solve other people's problems. I think that desire to eliminate barriers and to fix what's not working are qualities that define entrepreneurial personalities. It's the idea that you're never done growing. There's not a day that I don't wake up and ask myself what I could do better."

Invest in Relationships

Budziak has cultivated her professional network as carefully as she has grown her business. "Thanks to Don Dea, one of the contributors to this book, I had my first project helping him with an AMS selection project. From there I began working with other consultants as a subcontractor as well as gaining my own customers."

"As I was growing the business, I began partnering with a company Kevin had started, AssociationCIO." Then in 2010, .orgSource acquired AssociationCIO.

"Initially, we were focused on digital strategy and vendor selection," notes Budziak. "But as those activities became increasingly intertwined with management and operations, we started fielding requests for support with a broader range of services. We saw our colleague Sharon Rice's departure from APICS, the Association for Supply Chain Management, as a great opportunity to leverage our deep technology expertise with her deep experience in the areas of strategy and business development. This has been a natural evolution into an integrated approach to planning that acknowledges the disappearing borders between technology and other lines of business. The ability to put all the moving parts together and help organizations make the leap from goals and objectives on a piece of paper to successful programming has been extremely rewarding."

Fill Gaps Where You Find Them

Entrepreneurs are always searching for the gaps. They listen closely to their customers and the market to learn where they can ease a pain point or meet a need. That willingness to dive into a problem and solve it has characterized .orgSource's journey. "As we gained trust with our customers, we found colleagues coming to us for advice," Ordonez notes. "Sherry fielded calls in the evening or arranged coffee and lunch meetings with executives who were asking about everything from how to manage staffing issues to how to convince a reluctant board to upgrade critical systems. We began informally connecting our clients so they could discuss challenges together," Ordonez recalls. "The number of requests we were getting, for what often seemed like garden variety advice, made it clear that something was missing from the networking or educational support available. Sherry and I were both closely involved with many professional and volunteer groups in the community, and we asked ourselves where those experiences could be improved."

"Connection and innovation emerged as areas in which we felt we had something unique to offer," says Budziak. "Senior executives who were new to their positions and needed someone to confide in were calling me for advice. We were also working with large organizations in which there was a risk of failure unless they learned to navigate a more complex digital environment. Facilitating the exchange of knowledge among groups of peers and giving leaders the opportunity to learn from executives who were experimenting and forging new directions in association management were experiences where we felt we could offer value. .orgCommunity (www.orgcommunity.com), our networking and educational organization, was the result of wanting to meet those needs.

"We had started .orgCommunity in 2009 as an online-only community to provide executives to share knowledge. But the timing and the strategy weren't right to gain traction. So we already had some of the infrastructure in place when we decided to reimagine it in 2015. With help from our vendor partners, we were able to create a website and other technical assets. We surveyed our network to solicit feedback and evaluate interest," Budziak recalls. ".orgCommunity was re-launched in a matter of months. Over the last five years, we've been adjusting and refining the model in response to our constituents' needs.

"As a result of our activities with this new organization, another issue came to our attention," says Budziak. "I began receiving requests to help colleagues find specialized talent, such as grant writers and meeting planners. Simultaneously, I was getting queries from contract workers about whether I could connect them with employers. We began to consider how we might formalize those introductions. So another company, .orgFreelancer (www.orgfreelancer.com) was the outcome of that brainstorming. We have deliberately moved more slowly with this project so that we could test various options and assess what type of platform the community really needs.

"What I want to communicate most with this story about our growth is that evolution is constant. Identifying our customers' problems and building solutions is ingrained in our approach to business. We are not comfortable with inertia. We are always prepared to acknowledge a stumble and pivot toward a better outcome. There are many ways to solve a problem, and sometimes you need to try more than one strategy.

"I understand that a complex governance structure or outdated management model can impede associations from taking that more aggressive and agile approach to opportunity. But I believe that to succeed in the digital era it is imperative for organizations to become athletes. They need to begin building the flexibility to evolve and the muscle, or talent to best their competition, into their governance and operations. When I was developing business for AAD, I wasn't required to ask for approval at every step along the way. I was allowed to run with my ideas, and that made a visible difference."

Prepare for the Inevitable

Preparing for the inevitable transformation that is occurring in the workplace as a result of technology is top of mind for Budziak and

Ordonez. The shift in their business focus away from a linear approach to technology and toward integrated planning strategies reflects the movement that is occurring both in industry and the economy.

"We want to support our community's successful transition to Association 4.0 or the new business approaches that will be required to remain relevant," says Ordonez.

"The interest in .orgFreelancer is indicative of the changes to come," Budziak advises. "Finding the right talent is going to be challenging. Technology has given more people the tools to strike out on their own. There is a desire for greater work-life balance. Younger generations don't necessarily want to spend all their time in an office. We thought that if we could build a bridge between the workers with the skills and the employers who need them, that would help the association community thrive."

People are at the center of another area in which Budziak and Ordonez also believe associations need to prepare—technology. Ordonez says, "The organizations that are succeeding are the ones in which the staff embraces technology as a means of working more effectively. Not everyone needs to learn to code, but there shouldn't be anyone who can't pull information from their AMS, update a webpage, or use the email marketing platform. Hiring employees who are curious and eager to learn and making time to train them to maximize the resources available is critical."

"Business as usual is easy," says Ordonez. "But people need to make the effort to provide those extra staff development opportunities or give employees the space to learn new skills. Being outside your comfort zone should, and will, be the norm. In some organizations, there is the notion that technology is reserved for the IT department. That needs to change. Technology migrated out of IT years ago."

"Even organizations that are very tech savvy still may need to learn to strike the right balance between planning and implementation," Budziak cautions. "With innovation moving so quickly, there is the temptation to either rush to roll out new products and services or plan so meticulously that when the initiative finally launches it is already time for the next iteration. We have seen both approaches. Moving rapidly to make a quick profit without a fully conceived business plan will not provide the foundation for a sustained program. You don't want to be in the position of having to abandon a $50,000 learning management system because it wasn't what your customers were looking for. This is where the checks and balances and industry expertise that the board and committees provide becomes an asset rather than an impediment to progress. On the other hand, as an entrepreneur, I don't want to see plans linger on the drawing board. The competition both from within the association community and from for-profit organizations does not allow for innovation at a leisurely pace."

Create New Structures

"New business models are another inevitability that associations must be prepared to explore," says Ordonez. "As we've noted, the current association governance structure is out of step with an environment that is characterized by instability and the need for constant innovation. However, CEOs walk a political tightrope. Volunteer leaders may have spent years building the credibility and network to be nominated to the board. A CEO whose fresh perspective diminishes or changes the role they signed on for won't be in a good place when his or her contract is up for review. In addition, all of the volunteer leaders are temporary, so there aren't strong lines of accountability. While the membership could be seen as shareholders, they have no real skin in the game."

"H. Stephen Lieber, who contributed to our book *Association 4.0—Positioning for Success in an Era of Disruption*, is a great example of a CEO who navigated that challenging political terrain and accomplished a successful reorganization," says Budziak. "The Healthcare Information Management Systems Society created seven separate boards to each govern a specialized portfolio of products and services. Specific criteria to support that structure were developed, and subject competency is a fundamental requirement for leadership. Each entity was encouraged to avoid compromise and think about the future, and every business unit is accountable to a distinct set of metrics. It's a highly entrepreneurial model that positions the organization to mine opportunity across the widest spectrum of their market."

"Of course, that is a unique solution which would be challenging for many groups to emulate," says Ordonez. "But it demonstrates how one can rearrange the blocks to build a more successful configuration. Another option, which several of the contributors to this book recommend, is the idea of viewing an association as an incubator for innovation. Trade organizations are uniquely equipped to nurture invention. They have an intimate understanding of the issues in their industry."

Budziak agrees, stating, "Each time there was a leadership change at AAD, I was asked how the for-profit subsidiary fit into the mission. It was challenging to find a credible explanation besides the financial one. Had we presented ourselves as an in-house engine of research and development, that would have changed the entire perception and opened the door to more opportunity. We were not only having financial success but we were building products including one of the first learning management system, etc."

"The real value of this concept isn't financial," says Ordonez. "It's in having a brain trust for the organization and an incubator for intellectual property."

Be a Student

Approaching leadership as a student rather than a teacher is a trait that Budziak and Ordonez agree makes for a successful CEO. "David Martin, CAE, the CEO at the Society of Critical Care Medicine, was another contributor to our first book," says Budziak. "He is technically sophisticated and understands how that knowledge can impact every aspect of his business. SCCM is a completely data-driven association. Martin knows his customers and has built the infrastructure to provide the online journey they anticipate. He is constantly thinking about improving the digital experience based on customer feedback. Martin is successful because of his digital leadership and ability to foresee what SCCM's constituents will be expecting in the future. Martin had a vision in 1994 with the AANS to develop the first website for an association and continues to think about providing great digital experiences for the members they serve at SCCM. He learns everything he can about his constituents and develops a 360-degree view that encompasses all their touchpoints."

"Each of the entrepreneurs we interviewed for this book has a story about how they grew a business. No one was an overnight success," says Ordonez. "They all experienced bumps along the way and have shared the lessons learned. The humility to acknowledge that you don't have all the answers and to ask questions coupled with a healthy respect for the expertise of others both above and below you is critical. The Controversy and Comment—Topics for Group Discussion section at the end of each chapter in this book reflects leadership issues for a digital business environment and a lens through which readers can consider their own organizations."

"Lifelong learning is definitely a common denominator," says Budziak. "Everyone who is building a business is also improving themselves. The stories in this book illustrate that evolution is the essence of progress. Very little is perfect the first time out of the gate.

Success is a constant process of understanding what has worked, refining those strategies, and abandoning anything that doesn't contribute to your value. With every step forward, make time to pause and ask why your organization exists. Consider whether the vision you had two years ago is still inspiring enough to sell your mission without any other bells and whistles. If it no longer moves hearts and minds, put a blank slate in front of you and fill in the ways you need to change. Then have the courage to grow a stronger, more inspiring organization."

Topics for Group Discussion

Is your organization's vision compelling enough to move hearts and minds?

- If not, how does it need to change?

Where is the untapped talent in your organization?

- How could you leverage that expertise?
- What do you do to identify hidden talent?

Are there gaps in your market that should be filled?

- Where are your constituents' pain points? What products or services could address those needs?

Does your organization have the talent it needs to succeed?

- Where could you use additional expertise?
- Are you providing training opportunities that empower your staff to use the technology at their disposal?

How could your organization be an incubator for invention?

- Are there opportunities for you to develop intellectual property?

Meet Our Companies

Our companies are dedicated to supporting associations as they undertake transformative change. We provide strategic guidance, practical solutions and access to a vibrant network of executives and education opportunities to strengthen associations and the value they provide to society.

- Founded in 2005, **.orgSource** (www.orgsource.com) works with association to help improve operational efficiencies and create business strategies. From developing an integrated strategic plan to preparing your association for a digital future and supporting implementation of your important projects and initiatives.

- **.orgCommunity** (www.orgcommunity.com) connects association professionals to a vibrant network of executives, entrepreneurs, and strategic partners dedicated to shaping the future of associations. You can gain access to collaborative events, small group learning opportunities, and peer-to-peer counsel with trusted allies, mentors, and friends who share your passion for excellence.

- **.orgFreelancer** (www.orgfreelancer.com) makes it easy for organizations and freelancers to connect and get work done. Whether looking for specific expertise, short-term help to complete a project, or filling an opening while you recruit, .orgFreelancer can help.

Get to Know Sherry

- **My favorite people**— Are kind, dependable, trustworthy and hardworking.
- **I've always wanted to**—Make a difference.
- **My most memorable meal**—So many funny business trip stories and nice restaurants when traveling. One of the most memorable was in New York City at the Gotham Bar and Grill. (You will need to ask me about it). The Ritz in Maui.
- **I've always wanted to**—Be a better public speaker.
- **I'll never forget**— "There are three ways to ultimate success: The first way is to be kind. The second way is to be kind. The third way is to be kind." – Mister Rogers

Get to Know Kevin

- **My favorite people**—My family and those who have supported all my crazy ideas and business opportunities.
- **My most memorable meal**—Client and partner dinner at Gotham Bar and Grill in New York City.
- **I've always wanted to**—Visit the Great Wall of China and the Egyptian pyramids.
- **I'll never forget**—My first sales presentation (more than twenty-three years ago) at the first company I started. My demo system crashed on the plane ride to the customer, and I had to resort to a paper demo that had screenshots of the system interface. They are still a client today.

CHAPTER 2: DEA AND LEE

CONNECTING THE DOTS

Don Dea and Hugh Lee, Co-Founders and Owners, Fusion Productions

> *"Instead of managing a company, you're managing an ecosystem that is networked and connected over the world. Associations are, by their nature, networks. They're fluid."—Jim Collins*

Don Dea and Hugh Lee are natural synergists. They've been putting people, ideas, and innovation in the association community together for forty years. The partners have grown their business, Fusion Productions, by being canny observers of the environment and staying two steps ahead of the latest technology. Lee likes to say, "Life is about connecting the dots," and throughout their career, the two have never let go of the pencil that traces their progress forward.

Fusion Productions is a strategic meeting partner. The company has worked in venues across the globe creating conferences and events that generate excitement, engagement, and knowledge for associations and corporations in industries and professions from health care to manufacturing and all points in between. For the last twenty years, Fusion has also made digitalNow, the company's two and one-half day executive summit, a must for association leaders seeking to understand how new technology will impact their organizations, professions, and industries.

Maximize Opportunity

A talent for leveraging serendipity characterizes Fusion's history. Dea and Lee's introduction to the association community began with an unexpected invitation. The relationship might have been short-lived if the partners were less adventurous. As Lee recalls the experience, "In around 1977-78, I got a call from a staffer at the American Society of Association Executives (ASAE) who wanted us to speak at a conference. We discussed the topic, which was marketing and engagement. Then I asked about the budget. She admitted that, actually, they were inviting me to speak for free. But she immediately followed that news by assuring me that I would be exposed to the power of associations. I remember saying to myself, well this is quite a gig they have going.

"Fortunately, we decided to take a chance," says Lee. "Then Kodak, who was one of our big customers, introduced us to the Photo Marketing Association, and we began doing programming for that group. But the most significant breakthrough was something you couldn't possibly have planned. Ray Hall, who was the CEO of the Electronic Representatives Association, is a legend in our industry. I had been trying, without success, to get a meeting with him. The two of us were chatting during one of his general sessions and fell on the topic of vacations. I mentioned that my parents lived in southern France and that I'd been to Aix-en-Provence. Ray loved Aix, and from there our conversation took off. That connection launched our production, meeting, and design business."

Following their entry into the association sector, Fusion's involvement with ASAE continued to mature and grow. "We developed the first member survey that ASAE ever conducted," says Lee. "That led to leadership roles in chairing the Business Services and Associates Committee. Working with staff liaison Debra Sher, we tried to get ahead of the curve and created the first Technology Section. I think those innovations had an impact which very few people may realize. Today the ASAE trade show includes about 50 percent or more business and technology representatives, compared with years ago when hotels were the primary exhibitors. Many of the education programs developed as a result of taking a more business-oriented perspective. We also participated in creating the Strategic Leadership Forum and chaired the Association Think Tank event."

Lee and Dea take special pride in a study that was coordinated by ASAE and The Center for Association Leadership. "The project resulted in a book, *7 Measures of Success: What Remarkable Associations Do That Others Don't.* Business author Jim Collins served as a mentor to the research team. What many people don't realize is that the initiative was inspired by digitalNow," says Lee. "It was an in-depth, four-year effort with far-reaching implications for ASAE members and the sector. Don and I were involved from the inception in 2002 until the conclusion in 2006."

Watch the Market

The ability to seize opportunity has certainly contributed to Fusion's success. But a commitment to study the market and pick up on cues is also fundamental to Lee and Dea's approach as entrepreneurs. "When we started the company, we had over $1 million worth of business doing slides," Lee recalls. "Forty years ago that was worth something, but I was reading about how these things called personal computers and laptops were going to change the industry."

Lee understood that in order to keep the company on the cutting edge, he needed to act quickly. "I sat down with the staff and told them we had to be out of the slide business within the next 18 months. I said, 'We're going to replace that million dollars with a thing called PowerPoint.' We changed our entire model. You take a lot of risks, and you're never really positive that you're right. But you have to believe in yourself. Being an entrepreneur is about having the passion and nerves to endure the failures and leverage the opportunities without thinking about the cost."

A similar inspiration triggered the development of digitalNow. "Twenty years ago, I was sitting in a room with George Aguel, current President and CEO of Visit Orlando and a former Disney executive, and some other colleagues," says Lee. "Everyone was complaining that the dot-coms were coming to eat our lunch."

Significant changes were clearly on the horizon for associations, and the community needed to learn more about how technology and digital were going to impact business. "It was one of those lightbulb moments when passion for an idea grabs you," Lee recalls. "Don and I knew a lot of the folks on that side of the industry, and we were eager to organize a conference to address this phenomenon. We had the credibility and trust from our volunteer roles at ASAE. We just needed a venue. George agreed to provide the location if we would handle the content and the design." Twenty years later, technology is evolving faster than ever and digitalNow is still helping leaders manage and maximize innovation.

Reflecting on their success with digitalNow Dea notes, "One of the high points for me is the incredible group of people we've added to the digitalNow community. The colleagues who came to our first event took a risk in attending a conference they knew nothing about. At the end of the meeting when we closed everything out, we expected the crowd to leave. But so many people stayed behind because they wanted to help us shape the future. Most of those folks were young in their careers. Over the last twenty years, we've watched as they became managers, moved on to the executive level, and even stepped into CEO positions. They've really transformed their industries and sectors. From a professional standpoint, knowing that you've contributed to that growth is exciting and special."

When they reflect on their own personal development, Dea and Lee both credit their families for providing mentorship and motivation. "Maybe it's my Asian heritage," says Lee, "but the most inspirational figure in my life has been my father. Of course, my kids still straighten me out. I've learned so much from them. In my career, I'd have to say George Aguel, who co-founded digitalNow with us, and the author Jim Collins have had a big impact on my thinking. Our digitalNow Advisory Group is also incredibly influential. They constantly ignite a lightning stream of innovation. I'm excited by those relationships and by watching a project come to life. I think that's why I relate so closely to Jim Collins's work. You have to have the passion and find excitement to make that heavy flywheel turn through the momentum of your ideas—everything else is extraneous."

Pick Curious People

As much as Dea and Lee have been inspired by their colleagues, they have a legacy of moving others further along the creativity continuum. "In our business, we put our mission and our people in front," says Dea. "We focus on our passion and getting the best talent we can find to join our team. Making a difference in society is the common thread that brings us all together. That's why this journey is fun for me.

"An experience when I was at Xerox in one of my first executive positions taught me a valuable lesson about culture. I supervised a sales manager whose team consistently produced top numbers, quarter after quarter, year after year. One day at a recognition event, I asked him about the secret to his success. He told me that as a former schoolteacher, he always tried to hire other teachers for his teams because he knew that they would be eager to learn. Intellectual curiosity—someone who loves knowledge for its own sake—is a quality that we value.

"The other thing is trust," says Dea. "I had my own contracting company in college and realized very early on that when you agree to deliver a building or a home, people are depending on you. So, you have to hire people you can trust to follow through and execute."

Learn From Each Model

It stands to reason that Lee and Dea seek out lifelong learners. The company itself is constantly evolving and adapting based on the results of their work. "We are risk-takers," says Lee. "Each effort leads to something new. You move forward and you learn. One of our earliest projects was a large-scale model of a community platform. It was about five years ahead of its time. We were trying to research the potential of this new product, educate our clients about the benefits, and deal with a technology that was evolving. Given that confluence of issues, it's amazing how successful we were. From 2001 to 2002, we had nineteen communities.

"That experience helped us create better products. We discovered that you can't customize for everyone. It's impossible to manage nineteen versions of a platform when technology, the environment, and culture are demanding ongoing change."

Both Lee and Dea view a learning culture as critical to organizational growth, particularly for associations. They believe the world is changing too fast for leaders to adopt a passive, isolationist attitude. "Association executives have to see their entire ecosystem," says Lee. "They need to look beyond the tight-knit industry definition of the profession they represent to the bigger picture.

"Based on our research and experience, that more global perspective starts at the top. The digital age is all about leadership. It's the style of the CEO and executive team that drives the governance and the culture. Jim Collins advises, get the right people on the bus and the rest will take care of itself. You can have the best governance model, but with the wrong people on the team you won't be successful."

CEOs in the next decade, the partners agree, will need to thrive on diversity of all kinds—generational, cultural, professional, and intellectual. Jobs are changing such that it's hard to pigeonhole workers into distinct categories. "As an example," Lee relates, "several years ago we invited to digitalNow some young presenters who were developing cutting-edge farming technology. They were using drones to fly over fields and analyze the irrigation and fertilizer required by individual plants and crops. The information was transmitted to robots on the ground that provided the appropriate care. They didn't consider themselves in agriculture or robotics. They felt that, at that point in time, they had no professional home. This type of industry cross-pollination is going to make defining the future workforce very different."

"The concept and nomenclature around 'members' are going to have to be flexible, if not dramatically changed," Dea agrees. "Leaders will probably need to draw in influencers from the other disciplines that are affecting their organizations. Associations will have a role in helping their professionals navigate the friction that comes from this disruption and the introduction of new competencies and skills so that at the end of the day, whether it's a firm, a trade, or an individual, there can be a successful transition along a continuum as each level of competency creates a new category of belonging and affiliation.

"To help workers adapt, associations will need to find and hire terrific athletes—talent who can quickly build new models and leverage data to create products and services that didn't previously exist," Dea advises. "Over the last forty years, associations have relied on the notion of membership. Now I think they're going to be dealing with products, services, and education. The focus will switch from membership to product life-cycle management."

"To succeed during this time of opportunity," says Lee, "CEOs will need to be young at heart. There will be plenty of pins and needles and speed bumps as business shifts and changes. Passion and a sense of purpose about where they are taking the organization will be critical."

"There's a lot of discussion about whether leaders are born or made," Dea notes. "You can teach skills, but people learn values as they grow up through family, friendships, and life experience. So, society at large has a role to play."

"But Don and I both know," Lee advises, "that the most important ability is a bit elusive. It's a talent that develops from a combination of experience, training, and intuition. You need to pay attention, read the landscape, and see beyond the present moment. Success is all about connecting the dots. The world is full of opportunity, but you need to be ready to seize it."

Topics for Group Discussion

What does connecting the dots mean to you?

- Is there potential for synergy in your environment that you are missing?

What role does intellectual curiosity play in your organization?

- Are your teams encouraged to explore ideas for their own sake?

- Are questions welcomed, even when they might be disruptive?
- Do you hire people who love learning? How do you evaluate that quality during the interview process?

Do you believe that success rests with picking the right leader? Why or why not?

- Can great teams survive poor leadership? Why or why not?
- What can an organization do to mitigate subpar leadership?

Are leaders born or made?

- Which is more important: skill or character?
- What can be done to create more effective leaders?

Meet Fusion Productions

Fusion Productions is a leader in providing meeting design and production, media, and e-learning/online education to the association market. In a time of multidisciplinary and multigenerational audiences, the company collaborates with teams to rebrand, redesign, and produce meetings that engage attendees.

Fusion's e-learning group provides multiple level options to leveraging subject matter experts (SMEs), current content, assets, and conference material to deliver value and revenue opportunities 24/7.

Get to Know Don

- **My favorite people**—My parents (Kim Fun and Moy Sieu)—immigrants who imparted the importance of faith and education; and my wife Catherine, daughter Erin, and son Alex.

- **My most memorable meal**—Having a private dinner with Catherine on Ka'anapali Beach in the pouring rain with just an umbrella, a table, the ocean, and a waiter at the Hyatt Regency Maui.
- **I've always wanted to**—Make a difference in society and at the same time work with people who I want to be with. It's a life lesson from my parents.
- **I'll never forget**—Our son Alex's election as student body president at both McQuaid High School and Boston College. At his MBA graduation at the University of North Carolina at Chapel Hill (UNC), he was recognized with the UNC Kenan-Flagler Outstanding Leadership Award. Nor will I forget serving as Special Assistant to the Attorney General, Department of Justice, as Xerox's representative to the President's Commission on Executive Exchange Program or spending 4 months in the Massachusetts Institute of Technology Senior Executive Program with an incredible cohort of business leaders and friends.

Get to Know Hugh

- **My favorite people**—My mom and father, Ruth and Gim Lee, daughters Alexandria and Francesca, and wife Grace.
- **My most memorable meal**—The first time I treated my Mom and Dad to a dining experience at the Le Capitaine in Saint-Jean-Cap-Ferrat, Alpes-Maritimes, at the age of 26.
- **I've always wanted to**—Take the family on a summer vacation to see the national parks.
- **I'll never forget**—My father saying, "If it's worth doing, it's worth doing right!"

CHAPTER 3: VANDAMME

DRIVEN BY THE CREATIVE ITCH

Sigmund VanDamme, Membership Software Evangelist, Community Brands; Founder NimbleUser, Enterprise Association Management Software

> *"I've missed more than 9,000 shots in my career. I've lost almost 300 games. Twenty-six times I've been trusted to take the game's winning shot and missed. I've failed over and over and over again in my life and that's why I succeed."—Michael Jordan*

For almost as long as he can remember, VanDamme has had the itch. "Entrepreneurs need to create—to build something new," says VanDamme. "When I was single, I had a roommate who was a really smart guy. He was getting his master's degree, and his nose was always buried in a book. One morning at breakfast, his expression was especially intense. When I asked him what was so interesting, he told me he was studying to be an entrepreneur." VanDamme pauses to enjoy the irony of this statement.

"My brother and I were hustlers. We didn't come from a wealthy family. Our parents were immigrants. If we wanted spending money, we had to earn it. We plowed snow, mowed lawns, and were moguls of the Rochester, New York, paper route circuit. It was a game for us. We were always trying to figure out what we could sell next.

"I've met lots of people who say they want to start a business. But very few do. You need the guts to risk everything." For VanDamme, that attitude distinguishes the managers from the entrepreneurs. "Good managers," he notes, "want to focus on consolidating market share or building a brand. An entrepreneur's first impulse is to get out there and sell." Of course, it's not a sustainable approach. While the rainmaker is scoring sales, someone needs to make sure the systems are in place to keep all those new customers happy. When VanDamme met his wife Dawn, he also found that partner who could help him take a fledgling software business to the next level.

Seize Opportunity When You Find It

VanDamme began his career as a software developer for Kodak. Early in his professional life, he experimented with a variety of tech and sales jobs. His entrepreneurial journey was launched when he and his brother were hired by the Dansville Chamber of Commerce in Dansville, New York, to automate their business systems. Investigating options for the Chamber led the brothers to discover iMIS, one of the first association management systems (AMSs) to rapidly gain popularity. "We were blown away by the fact that you could write the code once and the software would operate on both a MAC and a PC. A graphical user interface, which today wouldn't be worth a glance, at the time was awe inspiring."

The system turned out to be too expensive for the Chamber, but VanDamme was hooked on the product. After research revealed that there were almost 400 associations in the Rochester area, he was on the phone pitching himself as a dealer. He couldn't afford the $10,000 price tag, but he managed to talk ASI, the manufacturer, into feeding him leads. "iMIS took off, and VanDamme and Associates rose with them," he says. As time went by, VanDamme grew restless to return to his real passion—software development. When Dawn joined the business, VanDamme was able to refocus his attention on being an innovator. He wrote a bulk messaging product called Communicate for iMIS. Users could email, fax, and print labels from the same platform. Robust sales allowed VanDamme to invest in his business and hire more employees.

Like many companies that grow rapidly, iMIS began struggling to maintain quality. Users were frustrated with bugs in the software, and resellers like VanDamme were tired of putting Band-Aids on problems and hoping for the best. VanDamme and Associates made the bold decision to create a replacement for the iMIS E-Series. It turned out to be the right move at the right time. The product, which was called VanGo, was a hit with disgruntled iMIS users. Eventually, ASI came calling and purchased VanGo. As an entrepreneur with a couple wins under his belt, VanDamme was energized and eager to move on to a new adventure.

That moment came when Marc Benioff, the founder and chairman of Salesforce, the giant in customer relationship management software, announced that the platform would open to developers. VanDamme thought he had hit the jackpot. Writing their own association management software was a personal and a company vision. The option to use the salesforce architecture as a jumping off point finally put this goal in the realm of financial and technological possibility.

Match Dreams to Resources

"We planned to dominate the small association market," says VanDamme. NU Members, the product they created, was fully loaded with features that had previously only been available to much larger customers. It even won Salesforce's Top 40 Award, gaining its happy creators a trip to San Francisco, California, to demo the software to the Salesforce community. VanDamme and his team were certain the software would be a game changer.

When the time came to put NU Members through its paces and show off the streamlined dashboards and process automation tools, instead of expressing wide-eyed wonder, customers yawned and asked whether they could print tent cards and labels. After the first few demos, the team realized that they had created a Ferrari for users who wanted a Honda. Instead of leaping off the shelves, NU Members became a dust catcher. Not one system was ever sold.

The team went back to the drawing board to rescale the program to sell to larger organizations with needs that were a better fit for the software's features. It took an additional five years of development but in December 2011, Nimble AMS, a system built on the Salesforce platform, was launched. "NU Members was a huge error. But eventually, that failure took us down a path that we could leverage," says VanDamme. Nimble AMS was the result of those lessons learned. The new product's success led to its 2017 acquisition by Community Brands, a market leader in providing cloud-based software to associations, nonprofits, faith-based groups, and K-12 schools.

Use Failure to Grow Success

Every entrepreneur worthy of the name has a NU Members story. Failure is a rite of passage. Curiosity and the courage to experiment are part of VanDamme's DNA. "My mom was a huge inspiration for me. She was always willing to take a risk. My brother and I went to a Montessori school, and our mother was so impressed by the method that she moved us to England so that she could study to become a Montessori teacher. She was never afraid to try something new, and she encouraged me to do the same."

As an entrepreneur with an association customer base, VanDamme is acutely aware of the differences that characterize the two mind-sets. "Associations are risk averse. They want every project to be a home run. That's an unrealistic expectation." The paradox is that a culture that can't tolerate failure won't produce innovation."

VanDamme understands the kind of courage that is required to be a risk-taker in the association world. Some leaders address the problem by dedicating a portion of revenue specifically for experimental projects for which there is limited expectation for success. Others find confidence in getting a series of small wins before a big leap. But even with deep pockets, association CEOs always face the scrutiny of boards and the real possibility of being shown the door if they are unable to manage their volunteers' expectations.

Building an environment in which failure is not just tolerated, but expected, is a challenging proposition. But it is essential for meaningful growth. "You have to be able to convince others that the biggest risk is in doing nothing," says VanDamme. "When I hire new employees, I tell them that if they don't fail, they don't belong here. We expect them to push our envelope. Not every project is going to be perfectly executed on the first try. You have to be willing to take ownership of both your successes and your mistakes." VanDamme sees progress in analyzing errors, discovering solutions, and then moving forward.

"Humility was one of our core values at Nimble User. Nothing great gets done by one person. You can design the best software in the world, but if Joe doesn't sell it, or Dave doesn't support it, or Diana doesn't do the billing, it's going to be a failure. I coach a hockey team. At the end of each game, we do an exercise called Windows and Mirrors. When we win, each player describes a window, or how another teammate contributed to our success. When we lose, each shares a mirror or a suggestion for how they personally could have played a better game. It's a way to directly experience the impact of group responsibility.

"Preparing a board to tolerate risk is a sales process," says VanDamme. "To convince you to buy from me, you must believe that I can increase revenue, decrease costs, reduce cycle time, enhance the member experience, and finally, mitigate risk." Leaders must be able to communicate each of those points to both staff and volunteers and present risk within a cognitive framework. "I have a friend who is a scientist in a large engineering company," VanDamme recalls. "The organization has a multilayered process for innovation. The first step is intensive brainstorming. Hundreds of ideas are generated. Then each concept is tested against a series of predefined criteria until only the most viable remain on the table. I don't see many associations doing that type of vetting," says VanDamme.

Hire Great People, and Let Them Run

For VanDamme success lies in building a strong team, having confidence in their skills, and expecting that they are going to make a few mistakes. "You've got to trust people," he says. "I might choose to do a project differently than some of my staff, but their results are generally as good or better than I could have done myself. Our goal is excellence, not perfection. Above all else, we focus on the customer's expectations. If we make a mistake, we correct it, and we stand behind what we agreed to deliver."

Even high-performing teams struggle to keep up with all the technological changes that are impacting the association community. VanDamme's partnership with Salesforce is one way he stays in tune with mega trends in the industry. His eyes are on the subscription economy, personalization/tokenization of membership benefits, and seamless financial transactions as areas for major growth and change. VanDamme cautions, "Organizations that want to keep pace are going to have to provide what members need before they know that they need it—or zero click ordering."

VanDamme doesn't advocate adopting technology simply to be on the cutting edge. But he believes it's critical to take advantage of new techniques to constantly improve service. "Artificial intelligence can be very valuable in providing personalized member experiences. I'm surprised by how many associations are not using persona-based marketing to look at non-members and identify which of them could be converted by moving them through various stages of engagement. The point is not the technology, but whether you are using those tools to build success."

Be Bold to Win the Future

When asked to assess the future of associations, VanDamme is guardedly optimistic. "I think there is going to be greater consolidation," he advises. "There are some organizations that are stuck putting out fires instead of being able to change and grow. Those groups probably won't survive." Technology is already an inextricable component of operations. The associations that take the next step and incorporate a technological perspective into their strategic vision and planning have the best chances to thrive.

Credentialing is a unique niche in which VanDamme believes associations can dominate. "I see tremendous opportunity in the area of education," he says. "What other sector has the credibility to provide a trusted stamp of approval? With the cost of university education skyrocketing, certification will be increasingly valuable in the workforce." The CEO of the future will need the vision to discover similar innovative areas for growth and the courage to insist upon change.

In an increasingly competitive environment, leaders who are iconoclasts—who don't just upset the applecart but deliberately knock it over—will be at the top of every recruiter's list. The entrepreneurial itch will be an indispensable component of governance. Executives will need the drive to retool their organizations to fit emerging landscapes and the single-minded enthusiasm to bring others along with them on a challenging, but exhilarating, journey.

Topics for Group Discussion

How is failure viewed in your organization?

- What would need to happen to make failure a more productive learning experience?
- Do you agree that failure is necessary for growth?

How does your organization manage risk?

- Are there strategies you could implement to become more risk-tolerant?

Does your organization have a formalized process for innovation?

- Would identifying specific brainstorming formats be helpful?

Do you agree that the CEO needs to be an innovator?

- Why or why not?

Do you cultivate a shared sense of responsibility within your organization?

- What activities promote this concept?

Meet Community Brands

Community Brands is a leading provider of cloud-based software to associations, nonprofits, faith-based organizations, and K-12 schools. Organizations adopt Community Brands software to manage memberships, career centers, learning, accounting, mobile giving, peer-to-peer fundraising, donations, admissions, enrollments, and events. The organization has more than 2,000 employees, has 346 partners (not including subcontractors), and serves 100,000 clients in 30 countries.

Get to Know Sig

- **My favorite people**—Entrepreneurs Marc Benioff, Jason Fried, and Mark Mason. All have taught me to think differently.
- **My most memorable meal**—Was at Through the Looking Glass restaurant.
- **I've always wanted to**—Be a fighter pilot. It was a lifelong dream that I pursued until I realized it would not happen (and for good reason; I would not have been good at it).
- **I'll never forget**—The line between huge success and total failure is slimmer than you think.

CHAPTER 4: CEHRS

BUSINESS WONDER WOMAN

Adele Cehrs, CEO and Founder,

When + How Agency

"People do not buy goods and services.
They buy relations, stories, and magic."—
Seth Godin

Making magic for others sparked Adele Cehrs's ambition to launch her own public relations business. "Early in my career, I was vice president at a small agency," she recalls. "I was being showered with compliments for the new business I delivered. But all that rain wasn't growing my paycheck. When I landed a $500,000 client, my boss gave me a $1,500 commission. Then she took me to see the vacation retreat she was building. As we stood on the terrace admiring the view of the lake, she turned to me and with a sweeping gesture said, 'This is all because of you.' That did it! If I could build her a lake house, I was fairly sure I could build myself a company." When the

Washington Business Journal called Cehrs a "wonder woman," she knew she had made good on that promise.

Initially, Cehrs's family didn't share her enthusiasm for going it alone. "My mom and dad thought I was crazy. My grandparents were entrepreneurs. Between the four of them, they owned a bakery, a dry goods store, a bowling alley, and a penny arcade. My parents saw how hard their own parents worked, and they weren't totally wrong about my decision. I don't glorify entrepreneurship. It's a hard road. You have to have delusions of self-confidence and believe so completely in your skills that you are 100 percent certain you can bring something to market that no one else can."

Be Guided by Experience

With a goal of independence in mind, Cehrs made a move to a large international agency. Her plan was to gain experience working with the heavy hitters before striking out on her own. However, it wasn't long before that irresistible inner voice was urging her to leap into the ocean and swim with the sharks. When she told her husband she was turning her back on Madison Avenue, he had lots of annoying practical questions, such as: Did she have clients lined up? How about a business plan? What was her market position? Her conviction that she would figure it out wasn't the answer he was looking for. However, when she landed a Fortune 200 chemical company as her first client, he came on board.

Establishing a nonprofit niche for her business was the result of trying on the association hat and finding that, although she admired the style, it wasn't a good fit for her. "When I came to Washington, D.C., as a fledgling communications professional, I didn't know what an association was," she says. "It was during the housing boom, and I got recruited by the National Association of Home Builders. I had been working in the agency world, and I couldn't get used to the slower pace that the need for multiple sign-offs created."

It wasn't long before Cehrs switched back into corporate overdrive. Later, when she started her company, she realized that her association experience had opened a window into this segment of the market. Additionally, there weren't many public relations agencies servicing associations. Cehrs was eager to fill that void and help her clients do a better job of catching that coveted media attention.

Trust but Verify

Growing a company from scratch is a little like taking care of a baby. For a while, at least, it's pretty much 24/7. "There are crazy days when you feel like a glutton for punishment," Cehrs notes. "But there are also moments of pure joy." Nurturing a business and a family at the same time presented Cehrs with some unique challenges. As she was trying to straddle the two worlds, she discovered that even a foothold in both sometimes isn't enough to keep the business on track.

"I returned from a four-week maternity leave to find that a once trusted staffer had started his own agency in my office. It took me a while to recover from that blow. I set up different processes. Now, I don't manage so trustingly. This happened four years ago, but it stays with you. On the other hand, the failure didn't get me down. I picked myself back up and kept moving forward."

Cehrs also learned to be more selective about her clients. "Risk is always there," she advises. "When I started out, I was so happy that someone was willing to pay me for doing what I love. It was difficult to turn down business. This can be a major misstep. One of my first clients was a little-known cupcake shop in Georgetown. When we negotiated the contract, I framed my offer around the idea that I was going to help them be successful, and they would take me with them on that journey.

"My strategy to move their display counter closer to the door to create a line that would extend into the street was successful beyond even what I could have imagined. Ten years later, the line is still there. They developed a national reputation and even bagged a TV show. They also decided that to match that successful image, they needed a Hollywood PR firm. That experience made me structure negotiations differently. To avoid the lopsided contract syndrome, it's important to invest in a good lawyer early in the life of your business. It will be money well spent. I will say that I'm not sure I would have done things differently. because I've learned so much from my missteps."

Use Risk to Grow

Skiing the double black diamonds comes naturally to Cehrs. Being a risk-taker has helped her grow her business. "I really wanted to organize my own conference in New York City. As a journalist for *Inc. Magazine*, I knew so many outstanding corporate communicators, I wanted them all to have an opportunity to network and share with each other." Initially, Cehrs wasn't sure how she would find the funding and other resources for her first event, which she christened Binge Marketing. With luck and perseverance, she was able to recruit a sponsor who donated a prime Manhattan peak with a 360-degree view as a venue. "The planning was crazy and fun. But as the day drew closer, I was paralyzed with nerves. I kept imagining that spectacular setting with me as the only person admiring the view. I called a friend, and she gave me advice that I use to this day. She told me to relax and visualize everything working exactly as planned and then to make that vision reality. I followed her suggestion, and the conference went off without a hitch."

Cehrs is currently in the middle of another, much bigger, leap. Her goal is to sidestep disruption she sees on the horizon. "I believe that public relations is at a tipping point. If I continue business as usual, I'll be obsolete within five years. I must change my strategy to meet the demands of the future market. I'm preempting what, I think, will be a shake-up in the way agencies interact with their customers. My book, *Spike Your Brand ROI: How to Maximize Reputation and Get Results,* deals with the science and art of timing communications, a topic that fascinates me. I am repositioning my services around that concept.

"This wasn't an easy decision. I have some of the same concerns I had starting out twelve years ago. When you hit the reset button, the fear comes rushing back. Fortunately, I'm able to use those feelings as fuel. Fear is a motivator for me. I need it to be innovative."

Don't Get Comfortable

Most association leaders don't value fear in the way that Cehrs does. "Associations are not the best environment for people with my personality type. Entrepreneurs are more likely to be consultants and others who service the industry. The association world is not a culture in which we thrive. We want to be creative and to have our ideas realized quickly." Cehrs sees the hierarchical governance structure as an impediment to innovation. She also thinks it may serve as a crutch to preserve the status quo.

"Board members are recruited because they are leaders in the moment. Expecting them to be innovators is a contradiction. It's tough to think beyond current success." Cehrs sees the desire for achievement as a powerful motivator. "People who are still striving to get to the top will be the most future oriented," she says. The board does not have the inspiration to move beyond their comfort zone. The executive director, who depends on the board's endorsement to keep their job, creates yet another roadblock. The situation becomes an infinite loop. "That's one of the reasons why the structure needs to include outsiders," Cehrs advises.

Designating special groups as incubators for innovation is a strategy that could break the chain of complaisance. "By integrating innovation into the fabric of the organization associations can move beyond what they envision as possible," says Cehrs. "I'm not suggesting that the mission isn't pivotal, but the best business practices can advance that goal in new ways."

Cehrs acknowledges that associations fulfill an important cultural and economic role. But they need to use technology to improve the public's ability to experience their brands on multiple levels. "For example," says Cehrs, "if I want a coffee at Starbucks, I can order it on my phone and pick it up without interacting with anyone. On the other hand, if I want to sit by the fake fireplace, have a chat with the barista, and hear some easy listening jazz, that's available too. I can relate to the brand on my own terms. Starbucks is not dictating my behavior. Hilton offers another take on this concept. If you are a rewards member you can check in and have access to your room on your phone and completely bypass the reception desk. In order to retain their privileged place in the market, associations must offer their members a similarly broad range of choices."

Associations, Cehrs recommends, should focus on studying how consumers are interacting with their favorite brands instead of creating an experience and then hoping their members will enjoy and adopt it. They can learn from the marketplace and from vendors who invest considerable time and resources in understanding their customers. Associations need to look more broadly at the external environment.

Staffing is another area in which a more expansive perspective would be beneficial. "I think associations could be more creative about where they are finding new hires," notes Cehrs. "While it's great to know your industry and there's no doubt that the CAE is proof of that accomplishment, talent and a fresh set of eyes can also be an effective strategy to introduce creativity into your organization."

Seek Success Over Approval

The CEO's behavior gives permission for others to approach their work from an original perspective. "If we're all singing the same song," says Cehrs, "we're not moving forward. I hate seeing my friends who are taking CEO jobs be more focused on pleasing the board than on doing what's best for their association, their staff, and the profession. They imagine that they won't be employable if they resign or are dismissed. We have to change the culture that celebrates longevity into one that recognizes accomplishment. If a CEO was only in place for two years but realized a 30 percent increase in membership, that person is valuable. Even if the board pushed them out because they couldn't stomach the change, we should still be celebrating a CEO who was able to move the organization forward. That's a mind shift that needs to happen." Cehrs believes leaders should identify board members and champions who will encourage them to do their best work. Peers can be judgmental and contribute to the limiting attitude. "I've seen CEOs talk each other down from smart ideas," she says.

The future is going to require that associations do an about-face. By continuing to look inward, they risk implosion from a stubborn unwillingness to face the significant changes their constituents are already demanding. Leaders need to scrutinize the broader business community and adopt a more competitive stance. "Chutzpah is what drives me and other entrepreneurs to keep reinventing ourselves," Cehrs laughs. "If you could bottle that, it would be a wise idea for association CEOs to take a long drink."

Topics for Group Discussion

Are there signs of disruption in your organization's industry?

- If yes, how could you change and strengthen your position?

Has fear of the board's disapproval kept you from making necessary changes?

- How could you manage that situation more effectively?

Do you agree with the idea that people who are still striving to get to the top will be the most future oriented?

- How does that statement impact your organization?
- How could you identify board members who are future oriented?

Could your organization benefit from channeling fear productively?

- What are some of the issues that cause fear among your members?
- How could those challenges be used to drive productive behavior?

Meet When + How Agency

When + How believes the industry has reached a tipping point. The lines between marketing and public relations are increasingly blurred. Whether one calls it earned, owned, or shared, marketing has taken over social media, with public relations as a subset. Even the name of the profession has changed. Currently, terms in use include influencer marketing, media management, and corporate communications. But whatever the services are called, the name of the game is speed. That's why When + How built its business model around the science of timing.

Get to Know Adele

- **My favorite people**—I had the great pleasure of knowing John F. Kennedy, Jr, when I worked for his magazine in New York City twenty years ago. He was an inspiration to all who met him and certainly inspired my career in journalism and public relations.
- **My most memorable meal**—Wild boar in Tuscany.
- **I've always wanted**—To skydive. It's on my bucket list.
- **I'll never forget**—The first time I spoke at the United Nations. It was truly one of the highlights of my career.

CHAPTER 5: MARSICO

CONFIDENCE AND BOOKS GROW A COMPANY

Sandy Marsico, Founder and CEO, Sandstorm Design

"Some people say that I have an attitude—Maybe I do. But I think that you have to. You have to believe in yourself when no one else does—that makes you a winner right there."—Venus Williams

Novels, nonfiction, biographies, and everything in between have a place in Sandy Marsico's library. The titles accumulate because Marsico loves to read. When she decides to learn a new skill, she picks up a book.

"Before I owned a business, I thought being an entrepreneur meant freedom," she says. "I was 24 years old when I started Sandstorm. I didn't have grand plans. I just wanted to try and make enough money to avoid having a real job. After Marsico called her parents and told them she was going to start a company, she bought some books. She taught herself how to code HTML, became a search engine optimization expert, and studied the steps in building a business from the ground up.

"I didn't sleep," she says. "I read everything I could, and then I designed and optimized my website." Within 24 hours Marsico landed her first client from a Google search. Sandstorm Design, Marsico's company, has grown from a one-person show to a global digital brand experience and technology agency with more than thirty employees. The business specializes in designing and building data-driven websites. Her relationship with that first website lead, CareerBuilder, lasted over a decade and was instrumental in her growth.

As Marsico's career has matured, so has her perspective on the meaning of being an entrepreneur. "I haven't felt freedom," she says. "That was an illusion. I'm free to dream and to create. But my team and my clients are among the many people I answer to. When you are in a service business, you don't own your calendar."

Instead of the carefree lifestyle she imagined, Marsico found that the responsibility to oversee her business meant getting comfortable with risk. "You need the courage to take chances and the stomach to handle anxiety. With a growing business, things change, but they don't get easier." For Marsico, self-confidence eases the butterflies and clammy hands that come with making a leap of faith. "You have to believe in yourself," she advises. "You're the one who drives success and encourages others to follow. You're the leader, and you're also the only one who can't give up."

Commit to Lifelong Learning

"Everything I've done has been self-taught," says Marsico. "I got my undergraduate degree in art. When I wanted to get a master's degree in marketing at Northwestern University, I didn't have the preparatory background. I bought a book on the GMAT and studied until I scored well enough to be accepted. I still feel like a kid who needs to buy a book to figure things out. The more the company grows, the newer it becomes. I tell my children that school is for learning how to learn. I don't care if they make mistakes. I want them to know how to study and how to find their own interests."

In addition to her reliance on books, Marsico sees her colleagues as an invaluable resource. "I'm a huge believer in peer advisory groups," she says. "I was a member of Vistage for ten years. Now I participate in the Women Presidents' Organization; C200, a collection of female business owners; and Tech Masterminds, technology CEOs who meet once a month to share ideas. I also have the special privilege of chairing .orgCommunity's Women in Association Leadership Circle."

These relationships are Marsico's source of courage and camaraderie. "I am inspired by every CEO I meet. I'm fascinated by how they overcome barriers and what they've accomplished in spite of challenges along the way. Each leader has a backstory, and they have all experienced risk. They've felt the same punch in the stomach that I have when you lose. They know what it's like to take a deep breath and dive in even though the water is freezing. I love hearing how they did it."

Be a Warrior

Marsico looks for creativity across her company. "I don't believe in hierarchy. Great ideas come from any part of an organization. We each have different experiences, and we travel different paths. One brain is never as smart as many." She likes decision-making to be a democratic process. "When an idea comes to the table, I work with a variety of people, both one-on-one and as a group, to ensure that everyone is heard as we develop the concept. That way, the entire team moves in the same direction."

Marsico's unabashed optimism sets the tone for an environment that is risk tolerant and innovative. She notes, "I can find the bright side in almost any scenario. I love connecting the dots, spotting trends, and solving problems. I'm passionate about encouraging others to do more than they believe will be possible. When someone tells me the goal is too high or the project too complicated, my answer is, 'You can do it.' It's just a matter of building confidence—taking baby steps. It is so rewarding to see others grow beyond what they imagined for themselves."

A crisis point in the company's history was the opportunity for Marsico and her team to identify Sandstorm's core values. "Ten years ago," she recalls, "I woke up one morning and realized that I didn't want to go to work." As Marsico struggled to understand why she wasn't happy at her own company, she realized that she needed to look in the mirror. "I kept asking what was wrong with my staff, and I realized that they were not the problem, it was my fault. I thought I could lead by example, and I understood that was not enough.

"I called a staff meeting. The agenda was *The Best Company You've Ever Worked For.* We had note cards and a big whiteboard. We posted and recorded everyone's ideas. I promised the group that I would make our vision reality. But I also told them that the unproductive behavior had to stop. It was a successful bargain. Our values grew out of that meeting. They are each important, but the warrior spirit is our defining characteristic. Being a warrior means that we are all in this together. No one is left behind. That extends to our clients as well. Once we form a relationship, we do whatever it takes to make good on our commitments."

Marsico says this concept plays out daily in the company. "For example, no one likes to be the last person working late in an empty office—especially when you could use another brain. We've made it a practice to offer help or simply to stay and keep a colleague company. The warrior spirit describes how we feel about collaboration and putting clients and our people first. We even have a Warrior Spirit Award. This month it went to our development team, which recently completed a massive systems upgrade."

In a company that values creativity, it's not surprising that curiosity is the second Sandstorm value. "We want people who love to soak up knowledge. I've hired lots of musicians and actors who taught themselves how to code. The focus is growing and sharing so that we can be better, both individually and as a group. We recently created Sandstorm U to formalize that concept. Every quarter we plan to teach a course that all staff members are welcome to attend. The topic can be anything from technology to finance or how to write a creative brief. Recently, we had a guest speaker on taking presentation and communication skills *From Boring to Unforgettable.*

"We work hard, but we love to have fun and we appreciate the importance of balancing work and life. So, that's the third value. We create opportunities to celebrate together." Marsico realizes that people enjoy work more when they are acknowledged for their accomplishments. "You Rock is our peer-to-peer recognition program. It's an opportunity to publicly applaud a colleague for personal or professional achievements—both large and small. I started this activity ten years ago; I imagined we might have about 100 You Rocks in a year. Today, I read more than 200 of these tributes in just one month."

Budget for Risk

Asking why opens the door to saying why not. Marsico believes associations could benefit from more frequent evaluation of existing strategies and greater willingness to alter the game plan. To adopt this flexible attitude, it's necessary to have the funding to match. "I have a budget line for risk. These are not contingency dollars. These funds are designated for experimentation. I don't always know how I'm going to spend the money, but when there is an opportunity, we are ready to seize it," she says. "I have another financial strategy that also helps us innovate. When I plan for a new executive level hire, I use profits from the year prior to mentally prepay that salary. That way, the first year is less stressful. It gives a new executive space to get up to speed."

Marsico accepts failure as part of an evolving business. "Small losses come before a big win. If an idea doesn't pan out, I look at it as putting me one step closer to success." She acknowledges that association boards are not typically comfortable with this attitude. Clarifying the possible impacts can be a strategy to help board members accept greater uncertainty. "I look at the worst-case scenario," she says. "If I can live with that, then I will proceed. When my business was new, I worked from home. But I had a vision for more. I took my life savings and invested it in converting my remote business to an office lease using my home as a personal guarantee. I also offered my first employee medical insurance and a 401k match of 4 percent to compete with bigger companies. The worst outcome was that I would have to start over. I was prepared to accept that because I wasn't happy with the current situation, and I had confidence in myself and my ability.

"I still take risks, but now so many people rely on me. I feel like I have a backpack filled with my team as well as their families who depend on their income. I was able to break through this barrier when I realized that the only unemployable person in this situation is me. No one wants to hire a CEO who has been an entrepreneur for the past twenty years. But all my people are highly employable."

When boards are brave enough to confront the unknown, the payoff can be substantial. "The National Association of REALTORS® has been our client for fifteen years. We had the privilege of watching them grow REALTOR® University, a project that was both innovative and enterprising, from the ground up. Their vision was to offer a master's degree in real estate. In order to launch a global online university, they created an entirely new organization," says Marsico. "It took courage to commit to a major investment with so many moving parts. But now REALTOR® University has expanded its reach beyond what we could have imagined."

Look Up and Out

As competition demands that boards take a more adventurous approach, Marsico sees their composition changing. "I predict greater diversity and shorter terms. The incoming generation loves to wear different hats. Board members and CEOs with decades of tenure will probably be a thing of the past." The rise of temporary and remote workers is already impacting business. Marsico sees this trend escalating. "Both members and staff will be switching jobs and shedding their professional affiliations more easily. Members may move from one organization to another. Associations will need to be less reliant on membership fees and more focused on products and services. As an example, the Association for Corporate Growth has an expansive annual meeting, InterGrowth®, that attracts both members and non-member dealmakers looking to grow middle market mergers and acquisitions."

The insular attitude toward membership spills over into staffing. Marsico recommends that associations search more broadly for talent. "Hiring from within the industry is common with associations. I love the collaborative nature of association work and the service orientation. But people with unique experiences can introduce breakthrough thinking. Marketing and technology are areas in which looking up and out is especially important."

How can leaders who aspire to the corner office prepare? Marsico's advice is, "Be visionary. Successful people at the top must be democratic enough to collaborate and inspire others, yet strong enough to take responsibility for difficult decisions. Transformation will be continuous, so it's important that leaders have that 'all in' warrior spirit. I'm already seeing some of these executives today, and I'm optimistic about the future of associations."

It's clear that associations must move beyond networking. They can change the landscape faster, and they can do it better than large institutions. "I'm proud of what the National Association of REALTORS® did," Marsico says. "They saw this trend coming and were brave enough to create a new model. I'm not suggesting that all associations start universities. I'm just saying there is a gap that is waiting to be filled."

Make Use of the Data

A culture of data is central to effective risk management and planning. "Weave data into everything you do. It brings objectivity to the table," says Marsico. "The source can be primary, secondary, or quantitative. Data is behind all our decision-making at Sandstorm. When we expanded our office space, we researched what our employees needed. We found that they wanted to be able to make their own meals at work. So, we built a chef's kitchen. Without the research, I would never have imagined that this was a priority. We also created an idea lab with plenty of dry-erase boards and corkboards as well as a library we fondly call Hogwarts, a soundproof, dark room with low lighting, comfortable seating, and a no talking policy. I built what my employees told me they needed. It's an example of using data—finding the gaps and filling them in."

Data delivers value, but people still rule the numbers. "Let's keep the focus on member engagement and experience," Marsico urges. "My favorite thing about associations is that they have the same fundamental purpose. They help people become better versions of themselves— to grow in professionalism and confidence. So many of us in this industry have that goal. We need to keep asking how we can share and give back. I believe that by providing great jobs to outstanding people, I'm making the world a better place. Associations do the same. We're all changing the world one job at a time."

Marsico's career is proof of the impact reading can have on life. What started with a few books has grown into a vibrant workplace that's changing the association community's digital landscape.

Topics for Group Discussion

Have you defined workplace values?

- If so, are you living up to those standards?

Would the Warrior Spirit be a good fit for your team?

- What does being a warrior in the workplace mean to you?

Are you using data to answer important questions?

- If not, what could you do to create a more data-driven culture?

What do you think about the National Association of REALTORS® project REALTOR® University?

- Are there gaps in the market that your association could fill?

How fluid is your organization's hierarchy?

- Do you seek ideas from all areas of the organization?

Meet Sandstorm Design

Sandstorm Design has been in business for twenty years and serving associations for fifteen. Approximately 20 to 30 percent of the company's revenue comes from associations. Sandstorm provides digital brand experience services, including brand strategy, research, data science, UX design, content strategy, digital marketing, Kentico and Drupal web development, web application development, maintenance, and support. Sandstorm's four practice areas are brand strategy, UX, web development, and data science.

The company has more than thirty full-time employees working in four locations (Chicago headquarters with satellite offices in Seattle, Charlotte and Denver). Thirty percent of the staff have worked for an association. Sandstorm's annual revenue range is $4 to $6 million.

Get to Know Sandy

- **My favorite people**—My family.
- **My most memorable meal**—Shark fin soup, in China.
- **I've always wanted to**—Go on a safari.
- **I'll never forget**—To continue to pay it forward.

CHAPTER 6: REHAK

WHERE LIMITLESS IDEAS GROW

Arianna Rehak, Co-Founder and CEO, Matchbox Virtual Media

"Leading innovation is not about getting people to follow you into the future, it's about getting people to co-create it with you."—Linda A. Hill

How do you grow a big idea? Arianna Rehak might tell you that transformational breakthroughs happen when you collaborate with interesting people and cultivate their thoughts. As the CEO and co-founder of Matchbox Virtual Media, Rehak knows more than a thing or two about making fertile ground for information and knowledge sharing.

Matchbox Virtual Media is a company that partners with purpose-driven organizations to produce virtual events which build knowledge communities around topics that matter. The company has built a methodology for virtual co-creation that meaningfully brings together groups of professionals and harnesses their collective knowledge.

Curiosity is Rehak's guiding light, and passion is the spark that ignites that flame. That journey began early in her intellectual life. "I started out studying business in university and then switched over to international development," she says. "I am fascinated with human nature." Rehak realized that development projects, which typically have an abundance of heart and ingenuity, sometimes fall short due to inefficient operations and misalignment of stakeholder goals. "Discovering that I could bring business acumen to that space and marry my two worlds was very exciting," she explains, "so it provided a useful lens in my studies."

Grow Knowledge Through Community

The online universe became the perfect playing field for Rehak's passion to collaborate, connect, and build community. "I got my start in the association industry with AssociationSuccess.org, a digital publication and online community for leaders in the field. I was hired to help drive the content strategy in the early months of the organization's operation. Participation in the platform's development gave me a sense of ownership over its creation, and I quickly fell in love with the association community."

Having a hand on the pulse of associations across the spectrum inspired Rehak. The quick flow of ideas, perceptions, and commentary was a good match for her own voracious appetite for learning. "Seeing the end result of what you are creating is a strong motivator," she notes. "Initially, our digital publication was meant to stimulate discussion within the online community. But the process began sparking creativity in the other direction as well. The community was generating ideas and feeding content to the publication. That synergy fueled my obsession with collective knowledge. I realized that when you bring people together to solve a problem, the final result is so much more powerful than what any individual could accomplish." She notes, "To embody this philosophy, you need to have a lot of faith in the strength and insight of your community."

The idea for the SURGE virtual conference grew from this concept. "SURGE was designed to capture the collective knowledge of the members of the AssociationSuccess.org community by gathering them under a virtual roof and engaging them around conversations that matter," says Rehak. Following the event, insights from the chat discussions and the presentations were repurposed as eBooks and articles that were published on the AssociationSuccess.org website.

"It's a bit meta to say this, but even the process of organizing the first conference was co-creation in action," Rehak recalls. "I got input from dozens and dozens of community members. I could point to multiple design aspects that resulted from advice I received along the way. So, my philosophy of development is certainly very bottom up."

Rehak's company, Matchbox Virtual Media, was a result of community feedback. She notes, "After SURGE was successful, attendees began asking whether we could organize similar initiatives for their associations. At first, we thought branching out would be a distraction. But the demand became impossible to ignore. We realized that SURGE was simultaneously filling a gap in the market and creating transformation. We launched Matchbox to meet that need."

Be More Than You Imagined

Rehak's work is very much an extension of her personality. "I have always been excited by learning," she says. "The first virtual conference was a result of my own intellectual curiosity, and as the Matchbox team grows, that inquisitive spirit keeps expanding. Recently, we were interviewing a potential new employee; he used the expression 'play with the data,' but immediately corrected with the word 'work.' In fact, 'play' was absolutely fitting for our culture. We delightedly hired him!"

Arianna brings a collaborative mind-set to all of her decision-making. "I have a habit of contacting at least five respected colleagues and friends who come from different backgrounds to give feedback on any idea. That strategy means that I can consider a question from several unique perspectives. I like to constantly turn stones over to see if a project is worth pursuing. The people in my close circle get frequent emails from me. That's part of who I am. The impact of that constant feedback is extremely energizing. It's also an early way to identify when an idea isn't worth implementing."

The vitality generated by collective knowledge is the defining quality of Rehak's work. Education events are typically venues in which information is consumed. There are knowledge givers and knowledge receivers, and there is a dichotomy between the two. In Matchbox virtual events, however, everyone has the potential to play both roles. Rehak notes, "Originally, we called our events virtual conferences, but we realized that the definition was limiting. What was actually occurring was co-creation. I like to call what we do a virtual, data-driven, co-creation methodology. That's a mouthful," she laughs.

Make the World Better

When the Matchbox team started out, they considered the values they wanted to promote. "We felt strongly that we wanted everyone in the company to be working their dream job," Rehak says. "That's been trial and error because the ideal work environment doesn't look the same for everyone. We're still figuring it out!

"To bring our vision closer to reality, we look for people who are hard-working and competent. But, above all, we want employees who get energy from making the world a better place. When we do our jobs well, we're making a positive impact and being enriched by the process," notes Rehak. "We're still in our first year of the journey. There are so many ways that we can grow and paths we can follow. My goal is to align our development with where people find excitement. That's involved a lot of experimentation, but we're seeing such rewarding results."

Rehak feels strongly that giving employees the opportunity to grow is important for their own success and for the company. "We want to recruit people who are currently not in positions where they have the opportunity to reach their full potential. That moment when people realize that their skill set and passions are aligning with value for the community is extremely powerful."

As a new model in the association space, innovation at Matchbox extends beyond staffing to many other aspects of operations. "Because we're blazing a trail, we need to be aware of where prospective partners fall on the adoption curve," says Rehak. "Embarking on virtual conferencing of this magnitude is a big decision for an organization, and so we have to be mindful of different comfort levels. The first organizations we work with are taking a larger risk because we're still in the iteration phase. What we've learned is you can't really stretch people much farther than where they naturally want to go. As we're building, we're lowering the barriers that might prevent the more cautious from getting involved and working with us.

"We have absolutely amazing partners who are early adopters. They are energized by an iteration process that would make others uncomfortable. Our early successes with them will mitigate the risk for others."

Cast a Wide Net

Rehak is a young entrepreneur building a new company in a fledgling industry, and flexibility and change are integral to her management style. "From one virtual event to the next, we're quick to find ways to improve efficiency or to question the energy we're putting into certain aspects of the operations," Rehak observes. This constant fluidity makes an interesting contrast to the association universe in which she operates. "I am struck by the challenge of initiating change in organizations in which decades of history and tradition can be barriers to experimentation," she says.

"When there are processes that have been in place for a long time it can be hard to see them through a critical eye. Familiarity makes it difficult to assess why you may not be achieving results or when activities should be sunset or approached differently. There is huge value in the curiosity to question everything. One piece of advice that has helped me is to take lessons from other industries.

"I was just reading a book co-authored by Ajay Agrawal called, *Prediction Machines: The Simple Economics of Artificial Intelligence*. It prompted me to invest in developing some technology tools in-house to make our processes more efficient. I'm quite certain that the only reason I came to this solution was because the book triggered a totally new thought pattern." Similarly, from time to time Rehak takes a 101 online course in an unrelated area. "Every profession and industry is solving for human nature under a different set of constraints, so there is almost always valuable application. You never know what taking an unfamiliar approach will produce. I think there is massive value in diversifying your thought patterns."

Feed the Excitement

Without that variety of ideas, organizations lose the ability to excite their constituents. "Enthusiasm dies when people are not able to get the right buy-in," Rehak says. "There can be many reasons why this happens. One of the major conclusions of an innovation study conducted by Amanda Kaiser was that the CEO's openness to new ideas has a huge impact on an organization's ability to change and adapt." Rehak also sees communication as central to the innovation process. "It's a nice challenge to figure out how to discuss change in a way that includes the goals of the person you are trying to influence. Aligning all stakeholders can be a complicated game of mental chess.

"Associations have the advantage of a built-in community. They are also good facilitators. When innovations are being considered, the group can be brought along on that thought process. The power of many can create the buy-in needed for changes.

"All our virtual events with Matchbox are centered around what we call 'the conversations that matter.' These are high-level, profession-wide discussions. We're picking up on trends across industries and professions. Automation is one of the significant topics that surfaces in many dialogues. A lot of professions are rethinking their roles in the changing landscape."

A recent virtual conference for certified public accountants (CPAs) provides a useful example. "Automation is fundamentally changing what it means to be a CPA, and that has major implications for members. It isn't just about reskilling; it also involves identity. It was important to our association partners that their members participate in the thought process of change. Virtual co-creation enabled them to shape their picture of the future together. It's also provided the associations with valuable insight into what their members are thinking and how they're reacting to the changes. At the beginning of the event, we polled attendees about how optimistic they are about the future, and then at the conclusion, we asked the same question. There was a noticeable uptick in reported optimism, which is huge!" Rehak feels that optimism is a key ingredient in embracing change.

Curate, Facilitate, Be Passionate

Engagement and consensus are skills that good facilitators bring to the table. "Look at Wikipedia or at Amazon with the community reviews," says Rehak. "The decentralization of knowledge is an important trend and one that I see as a valuable lesson.

"Leaders definitely need to be passionate about what they do, but they should also be skilled at co-creation and aligning common interests. When you bring people together to solve a problem, the end result will be stronger, and it actively engages stakeholders in the process.

"Associations are filled with people who want to make the world better," Rehak notes. "I think that there are many in this profession who have more to give and who want to put their energy toward great things. These are people who will be more engaged in their role if they are given bigger challenges and greater involvement. Having just spoken about the more negative aspects of automation, identifying ways to automate mundane processes in some jobs would free energy for bigger and better things."

As a resident of Montreal, Canada, Rehak has ample opportunity to stay current with activities in the information technology community. "We have two big industries here. One is video gaming and the other is AI [artificial intelligence]. Both significantly influence my thinking. Staying on top of technology surfaced as a common response when we asked our attendees what challenge keeps them awake at night," Rehak recalls. "I was a technophobe myself until I realized that technology is an enabler of really exciting outcomes. That completely changed my perspective. I felt differently about experimenting with new tools. Now if something I'm doing is boring, I'll try to find a way to automate the more tedious aspects. That's also the mind-set of our company. That's better for the bottom line, and it makes for more engaged staff."

Build Something Bigger Than You Are

"The German word 'gestalt' describes a process in which many small experiences, taken in totality, create their own unique phenomenon," says Rehak. "That's a good metaphor for co-creation. Dan Ariely, a behavioral economist who I really respect, studies how human behavior deviates from standard economic theory. As part of his research, he brought a group of people together to build IKEA furniture. He also asked them to value the pieces. When a control group was asked the same question, their estimate was 30 percent lower. One of the takeaways is that people who are directly involved in building something will perceive it to be of higher value. That example parallels my experience with co-creation. If facilitated properly, not only is it an engaging process, but the outcome will be more valuable to all the participants.

"A big part of my job has been to build community relationships," notes Rehak. "As a result, I've met so many incredible people. Once when I was sick and couldn't attend one of our early SURGE virtual conferences, I asked several colleagues to make sure the attendee chat environment was thriving and productive. They took on that responsibility in a touching way. Based on the influence and input of the people I've met, I proudly call myself a co-created professional.

Nothing excites me more than continuing to learn from the variety of opinions and voices that guide my adventures in this wonderful space."

Topics for Group Discussion

Are there opportunities for co-creation in your organization?

- Where could this technique be used?
- Would it be beneficial for your group?
- Do you see any drawbacks to this approach? If so, what are they?

What kinds of online interaction are occurring in your association community?

- Have they been successful? How would you define success?
- How could you expand on those opportunities?

What are the pros and cons of online versus in-person interaction?

- What is the appropriate mix of online versus in-person events?

How could virtual and in-person events be combined for greater impact?

Meet Matchbox

Rehak's favorite place to navigate to on the Matchbox website is the Our Team section. When she is having a rough day, she goes there to read the bios that were written by a teammate who now interviews every new person to capture their essence. Rehak considers it her great honor to be building this dynamic team and introducing them into the association community.

Get to Know Arianna

- **My favorite people**—Intellectually curious ones who value experimentation.
- **My most memorable meal**—Accidentally eating an entire family size portion of ribs by myself.
- **I've always wanted to**—Have the ability to whistle, though I suspect it's never going to happen for me.
- **I'll never forget**—The time I broke my arm trying to catch a football while jumping over a fence. It's good to remember the fallibility of human reason.

CHAPTER 7: PINEDA

GOING DEEP—A COMMITMENT TO SOLVING THE RIGHT PROBLEM

Joanna Pineda, Founder, CEO, and Chief Troublemaker, Matrix Group International, Inc.

"Problem-solving leaders have one thing in common: a faith that there's always a better way."—Gerald M. Weinberg

Solving a problem can be like eating an artichoke. Sometimes you must peel away lots of prickly leaves before you reach the heart of the matter. Joanna Pineda and her team at Matrix Group International, Inc., are experts at finding the sweet spot.

"We were helping an association client with meetings issues," says Pineda. "In the process, we learned that their conferences were a great source of new members, but retention was a problem.

(Attendees were automatically given a 12-month membership.) When we introduced the idea of an onboarding program to boost engagement, another aspect of the drop-off was revealed. People who attended a meeting in the fall didn't officially become members until January. By that time, the great educational experience was a vague memory. At the core of this counterproductive practice was an outdated system that made ad hoc invoicing difficult."

Matrix Group International, an award-winning digital agency that helps associations and nonprofits change the world, prides itself on going deep to discover where a client's real problems lie and fixing them. "I'm not a wheeler-dealer who is constantly negotiating the next new venture," says Pineda. "But if you describe an entrepreneur as someone who is passionate about scanning the marketplace and developing products and services that make people's work easier, that shoe fits me perfectly." Pineda has earned her entrepreneurial stripes reinventing her company more than once to reflect the changing technological and business landscape.

Pineda's early career was the inspiration for choices that would lead to business ownership and an enduring relationship with the association community. "One of my first jobs out of college was with the San Francisco Education Fund. We were raising money to support the San Francisco public schools. Experiencing the fulfillment that comes from serving a greater good shaped the way I think about working for nonprofits. My mentors at the Fund showed me the ropes about boards and governance. It was also an unforgettable introduction to sales. During an early pep talk, my boss said, 'Joanna, you're going to be selling something intangible; the benefits are a long way down the road. If you're successful doing that, you'll be able to sell anything.' He wasn't wrong."

Pineda went to graduate school and earned a master's degree in American foreign policy and international economics with her sights on a Capitol Hill job. Those plans quickly dissolved when she realized that her student loans could become lifetime debt on an entry-level policy staffer's salary. Instead, Pineda parlayed tech skills, acquired during a graduate school job at Ernst and Young, into a position designing bulletin boards (early versions of chat room/messaging systems) for the federal government and associations.

As an insatiably curious person who is drawn to innovation, Pineda was immediately fascinated with the emerging web technology in the mid-1990s. The transition from building association bulletin boards to designing their websites was a natural. "Associations do two things—they bring people with common interest together and they disseminate information," she notes. "The web was the perfect package to deliver both content and community. Many of our clients were paying for expensive public relations and media initiatives. We saw this as an incredible opportunity to skip the intermediaries and present the case directly to the public."

Strengthen Relationships to Build Success

"So many people have guided me on my career path," says Pineda. "When I was considering starting my own business, a friend offered to give me office space and to help me with the other logistics that would be involved. Enough people encouraged me and stepped up with support that I felt comfortable making the leap from employee to business owner. My sister Patricia sealed the deal with these words of wisdom, 'Well, if you fail, you're back to looking for a job, and you already know how to do that.'

"Some of the best advice I received was from Dan Walter, vice president and chief operating officer of the National Electrical Contractors Association. Dan has been a huge mentor to me and was one of my first clients. He said, 'The more you learn about my organization, the more you can help me. So, ask a lot of questions.'

True to his word, Dan always gave a straight answer. That forthright attitude has earned my immense loyalty and a passion to provide this organization with the right solutions when they need my advice. Dan is just one example of the many clients and others who have shared their wisdom to make me more effective at serving the association industry and running my business."

Be Uncompromising With No

Curiosity, determination, and the collaborative spirit characterize Pineda's leadership style. "I don't take no for an answer," she states. "This isn't because I'm trying to be challenging or difficult. I fervently believe that no matter how complicated the goal, there is always a way to accomplish it. When our business considers undertaking a difficult project, I don't wonder whether we can do it; I assume we can. The question I do ask is: In order to be successful, what needs to happen? That creates a different dynamic for assessing the situation.

"My faith in the power of creativity and persistence comes from experiences I had during college. I was fortunate to get a scholarship to Stanford. In my freshman year a friend told me that he wanted to take Gaelic but the university didn't offer courses. Undeterred by this small bump in the road, he approached the Foreign Language Department to see whether the problem could be solved. He was told that if he could get seven other students to take the course, the university would find a professor. So, when I had a dream of spending my junior year in Paris, but I hadn't studied enough French to be eligible, not to mention that I had no money to pay my expenses, I didn't give up. I spoke to my advisor and he developed a fast-track for me to get the needed French proficiency. After I jumped through all the hoops, the university agreed to pay for my trip. The experience taught me that if you are willing to invest time and effort in a project, people will often meet you halfway."

Data and opinion are critical to Pineda's deliberation process. "I take feedback from my staff on almost everything," she says. "It's not a democracy, however; there are some decisions that only I can make. But everyone has a voice." Pineda and her team also like to look long and hard at the issues and to gather as much pertinent information as they can. "I'm a data hoarder," she says. "I bookmark, I read, I make lots of lists. The downside to this personality trait is that people may think you're trying to micromanage. When I hire a new employee, I warn them that I ask a lot of questions. I explain that it doesn't mean that I want to do their job. I just need to know the facts."

Pineda's title, chief troublemaker, reflects her irreverent attitude and sense of humor. "When the company was new our designer snuck that into a draft of my business card as a joke." Pineda liked being identified as the innovator who keeps things interesting. Years later, she's still happy with that title.

Take a Fresh Approach

Welcoming new ideas is a hallmark of an entrepreneurial organization. Pineda sees a pressing need for associations to adopt a fresh approach. Organizations that are not entrepreneurial get saddled with outdated programs and technology. The technology debt is an especially insidious weight that prevents progress. "One of our clients was using a database that Microsoft has not supported for the last sixteen years," she said. "Getting them up to speed will drain resources from many other areas.

"We have several association clients who are struggling with disruption," notes Pineda. "It's clear that their success depends on reassessing strategy, yet there is considerable resistance to change.

Some groups report a slow but consistent decline in meeting attendance over almost a decade. Leaders need to watch these symptoms. The leaks have got to be fixed, or there will be major problems ahead."

Pineda is aware that many associations are reluctant to assume risk. She emphasizes that an entrepreneurial approach is more far-reaching; it's an attitude of acceptance and openness that generates excitement throughout the organization. This innovative orientation attracts the best people because they realize that they can achieve their personal career goals while contributing to your success.

Introduce New Perspectives

A culture that generates growth and responds to change feeds on variety. While an association's board may be demographically diverse, they are often far more homogeneous when it comes to professional experience. "I had an interesting conversation with a client about association boards," says Pineda. "He was considering the benefits of expanding representation to include expertise from outside the profession. Specifically, he suggested giving experienced association executives a seat at the table.

"If you don't have leaders with a range of professional backgrounds, there will not be a lot of new thinking. The average pharmacist, librarian, or dentist has limited experience with the challenges that are involved in running an association. It's a good idea to include people from outside your organization's playing field who can introduce a different point of view and push the group forward. The fact that association executives are still asking me my opinion about telework is just one example of why different perspectives are necessary. This issue is no longer up for debate. To question whether or not it's a good idea seems anti-trend. An organization that feels so archaic is unlikely to attract top talent."

The CEO, in particular, needs to be in tune with the larger business environment. "I belong to a CEO peer group called Vistage," says Pineda. "We meet once a month. Most of the members are running businesses larger than mine in very different industries, but our concerns are surprisingly similar. Association executives are really lucky. They can take advantage of .orgCommunity's leadership circle groups, where they can compare notes with executives who are on parallel journeys. The opportunity to share challenges, in confidence, with the brightest colleagues in the business is an invaluable resource."

Vistage contends that because the CEO has the biggest impact on the organization, he or she also is the person who needs to have the most expansive point of view and the broadest professional development."

The idea that the CEO is responsible for the health of the organization has been reinforced throughout Pineda's career. "Early in our relationship, my executive coach would remind me that every CEO gets the organization he or she deserves," notes Pineda. "If your employees aren't working well together and your office is siloed, it may not be because you created these problems, but you are the person who is allowing them to happen." Vistage, and similar groups, give CEOs a chance to benchmark their performance against peers across the business spectrum.

Educate to Innovate

In addition to building a strong team, continuing education plays a big part in keeping Matrix Group International up-to-date with emerging trends in technology. "We spend a lot of time on professional development and sending people to conferences," Pineda notes. The company also has a series of weekly meetings devoted to assessing the internal and external environment.

Employees who attend seminars are responsible for reporting back to the group and recommending how their learning experience could improve operations.

When an idea emerges that merits investigation, the team finds an appropriate test project that can serve as an incubator for the new venture. "It's expensive for us to have twelve people in developer meetings for an hour each week," says Pineda. "One employee probably spends several hours doing research and the person running the meeting also prepared for a few hours, but I feel like I have no choice. It's part of what keeps the company fresh."

Pineda and her team spend a lot of time thinking about the future of associations. They are especially focused on Netflix as an indicator of what's on the horizon. "Netflix knows so much about its customers," says Pineda. "They make highly appropriate recommendations based on what a person searched for and selected. Similarly, we believe that successful associations will invest substantial time and money to create a truly customized experience for every member. They will develop strategies to explore their content and benefits and curate the most attractive choices for each individual. In order to accomplish this, a cascade of other things should happen. Relevant data will need to be collected and effectively analyzed. Associations must be prepared to drop unnecessary activities and to invest in initiatives that may surprise them."

The strongest leaders are going to be people who know how to use the technology and data at their disposal to understand their members' problems and deliver solutions. CEOs must explore options with an open mind and be willing to consider a variety of strategies. "Several years ago, we worked with the Food Marketing Institute on a website redesign project," Pineda recalls. "They told us they wanted to have a better understanding of their members. When we completed our interviews, we discovered that the top two things members wanted were a curated experience and help with navigating the future. As a result, the association eliminated almost everything from the site that was not relevant to those objectives—or about 60 percent of the content. They also decided to significantly invest in better search capabilities to help their members easily retrieve the specific guidance they were seeking. That was a brave move in response to an honest exploration of what their members wanted."

Pineda believes that the old association model of yearly dues and big annual conferences is not sustainable. Younger members don't want an organization that was designed for their parents. She sees going deep—the Matrix philosophy of problem-solving—as a strategy that can help associations re-envision the future. "Change may mean adopting a gaming model, an entertainment model, or a nano model—which we are big fans of. All these avenues must be explored so that the core of what associations do—promoting professional excellence through community and learning—can continue."

Topics for Group Discussion

Is technology debt holding your organization back?

- How up-to-date are your systems?
- If you are using old technology, what are you doing to address the problem?
- If you currently don't have the resources to purchase updates, how could you streamline your current systems?

Do you have a process for evaluating programs to determine whether they continue to be relevant?

Are you making an adequate investment in your management team's professional development?

- How is learning shared across the organization?

How diverse in thought, experience, and demographics is your board?

- What issues are preventing greater diversity?

Do you and your team take advantage of mentoring opportunities?

- Do you have methods to benchmark your skills/progress against other executives in the field?

Meet Matrix Group International, Inc.

Matrix Group International, Inc., is an award-winning digital agency with clients across the United States. The company helps associations and nonprofits change the world. Matrix Group is fanatic about creating "Amazing Member Journeys" for its clients. The organization has forty employees in Arlington, Virginia, and around the country.

Get to Know Joanna

- **My favorite people**—My husband, Maki, my best friend Dayna, my two sons, and my martial arts master, Master Yun.
- **My most memorable meal**–Dinner in a tatami room at a ryokan (Japanese guesthouse) in Kyoto, during a trip to Japan in 2014.
- **I've always wanted to**—Go on safari in Tanzania or South Africa.
- **I'll never forget**—Getting married in the snow, skydiving with Maki, meeting Kevin Bacon, surviving my Tae Kwon Do black belt test, and my first million-dollar project.

CHAPTER 8: KING

MAKING BUTTERFLIES: THE POWER OF TRANSFORMATIONAL LEARNING

Tracy King, MA, CAE, CEO and Chief Learning Strategist, InspirEd

"What's dangerous is not to evolve."—Jeff Bezos

Long before Tracy King called herself an entrepreneur, she was fascinated with the visionaries who move business forward by nurturing an idea from concept to cultural explosion. "I was interested in their attributes and their skills," King says. "I wanted to learn what made them credible and what motivated them to start movements. I also saw that I had the seeds of those attributes inside myself.

"Starting a successful company requires more than business acumen," King advises. "You need to develop the right outlook.

Challenge should inspire curiosity instead of provoking defeat. You must look for options and seek to solve problems." As King grew in knowledge and experience, she also recognized that she had the muscle to build her own business. She began to work on acquiring and polishing those strengths.

Take Clients to Their Dream Destination

InspirEd, the company King created, guides associations to develop winning strategies in a crowded continuing education market. "You need to take clients on a journey to their dream destination. To me, being an entrepreneur means going beyond the symptoms of a problem and digging deep to identify underlying issues so that an elegant solution can surface," King notes.

Putting clients in that sweet spot requires continually testing the market. King has learned to embrace the concept of leading with the *minimum viable product (MVP).* Smart innovators begin with a prototype, a product with just enough features to be attractive, allowing customer response to guide the final design. This often means recalibrating frequently to meet evolving conditions. In other words, you don't jump to commitment, you wait for feedback to put a ring on it. King sees herself as a problem solver who is comfortable with making the iterative adjustments required to be both relevant and exceptional. "I create sustainability," she says. "And I never sit still, because neither does the marketplace."

Be an Agent of Change

When she began her association career at the American Academy of Neurology (AAN), King was already an established learning professional. "I'd worked in the corporate sector and academia," she says. "I was fortunate to land at an association at which innovation and delivering exceptional service were drivers. The leadership valued testing new ideas, and they embraced a healthy level of risk. I love facilitating conversations with stakeholders and separating the challenges from the distractions. AAN was an awesome place to use those skills."

King learned early that a great idea is the easy part of introducing innovation. To move beyond vision, you must bring others along with you. Articulating compelling goals and offering solutions for the disruption that occurs with change smooths the path. "As a result of my collaboration with a super professional staff and amazing stakeholders, I was able to successfully launch several groundbreaking programs at AAN," King recalls. "When I stepped into the manager of education role, my charge was to create a digital learning portfolio allowing a neurologist anywhere in the world to earn all of their CME [continuing medical education] credits online should they choose to. It was a huge vision that required we strategize our pathway to a tactical reality. The good news was we had a great engineering team to build the software. With their support, we nailed it!"

In a dynamic medical field like neurology, many physicians choose subspecialty training and certification to expand their practice opportunities. But because it typically takes twelve years to become a neurologist, adding additional education often requires physicians to put life goals on hold. In collaboration with the United Council for Neurologic Subspecialties Accreditation Council, King helped initiate a flexible fellowship. The new strategy provided an alternative option to meet subspecialty requirements while allowing physicians to practice part-time and enjoy better work-life balance. This was especially beneficial for younger doctors who were paying off student debt while juggling the demands of growing families or even eldercare. "We increased the number of accredited programs and participants because we offered a solution that allowed fellows to pursue their dream without sacrificing their personal lives," she says.

"While most of the education division focused on in-person learning events, my tiny team was responsible for digital learning. Each of our programs started with an idea that we nurtured into reality. People were curious because it was so different. I would often joke that we created awesomeness out of nothing." King's start in association management deepened her entrepreneurial skills within the multiple stakeholder structure of a membership organization.

Build on Your Passion

"I love facilitating transformation," King says. "That comes in many forms in my life—raising my children, coaching, writing, and in my work. Learning is the thread that ties everything together. I became aware of this at my first corporate job out of college. There was a skill gap in our team that was causing painful inefficiencies, and I knew how to solve it. I approached the vice president with my idea. She suggested that I develop a training. It didn't occur to me that she would ask *me* to do that. But as I dug into the experience, it felt electrifying. I was forever bitten by the bug.

"I went to graduate school and while I was working on my master's thesis, I was offered my first teaching position. I had taken a pedagogy class, and I had studied with incredible, inspiring instructors. I was eager to apply all my new skills." King arrived at her first classroom with excitement, a textbook, and an armload of overhead transparencies. However, it became clear it was going to take more than subject expertise and enthusiasm to engage her students.

"I quickly realized that I was a subject expert who didn't know enough about learning," she says. "My pedagogy class gave me a few tools, but I didn't know the *why* behind how to apply them. That experience inspired me to study the learning sciences. To motivate my students, I wanted to understand what was happening in their brains. My classroom became a laboratory. That's the foundation upon which my business is built. I did research and tested my ideas in the real world." King has continued to refine her research developing models for learning design, learning engagement, education strategy, and an innovation framework, making the best of the findings actionable for her clients.

For King, business ownership was a consequence of becoming an expert in her field. "A few years into my career at the academy, I began to miss teaching. I started to submit proposals and to speak at conferences," she relates. "I presented on the learning sciences, learning design, strategic innovation, and similar topics. After my sessions, people often approached me to ask if I could help them. When that happened several times, I realized that I was offering a unique perspective that was already in demand. I was marketable."

Assume Nothing

Like all new business owners, King took risks and learned a few lessons the hard way. "In my first year of business, I was working with a client that I was super excited about," recalls King. "We had a handshake agreement about what we intended to accomplish together and set our first deliverables deadline. Even though the contract was still in negotiation, I wanted to show them what I had accomplished. We met, I shared my work, they loved it, and then they walked away with the draft but without a contract. I quickly learned about negotiating fair agreements and protecting my ideas.

"Other risks I took revolved around prototypes that I tested, and the market returned a no. Each of those products was an elegant solution. They just weren't packaged to resonate with my ideal client. I learned to fine-tune my listening skills to create solutions that I could iterate to scale. Every time I test the market, it's an opportunity to discover a nugget that allows me to grow." King believes that association leaders can learn from this perspective.

Entrepreneurs can't afford to be snagged by the latest trends or cling to a proven business model because it's comfortable. "I've noticed a tendency in association management to make assumptions about the business environment. That's when you become vulnerable to disruption," King advises. "Executives are inclined to look outside for tips and techniques. You won't find the value proposition for your members by copying others. For example, some associations experimenting in the digital learning space are attracted to this technology for its own sake. But they have yet to explore its relevance to their members. The conversation should begin with your constituents and then branch outward."

That internal dialogue can't be an endless loop in which the same tired concepts are repackaged and served up as new. Creativity should drive these conversations. "Teams need space to innovate," King says. "Allowing for learning through failure creates the freedom to solve problems instead of checking tasks off a list. We must ruthlessly sift the challenges from the temporary distractions and seek the nuggets of truth in every successful disappointment. Incremental innovation is smart. So is listening deeply to the market and using MVPs to recalibrate. These are strategies that allow associations to see a real-time picture of their members' needs."

Risk assessment is another way for boards to be more comfortable with innovation. "When you discuss retirement with a financial planner you evaluate your tolerance for risk against the possibility of achieving your goals," says King. "This kind of honest conversation should happen at the board. Similar to the funds in an investment portfolio, lines of business can be weighted differently. You don't need to put all your resources in one bucket.

Drive Invention With Diversity

Changes in the workforce promise to make invention more accessible to associations than ever before. Millennials are eager to bring a fresh perspective to leadership roles. "They haven't been seasoned by years of experience, but that can be addressed through training, mentoring, and coaching. At the same time, there must be a heart-to-heart discussion about loosening the reins and allowing a new generation to bring fresh ideas," King advises.

Along with the introduction of a younger, more diverse leadership profile, the composition of teams is also changing. Workers are opting out of the nine-to-five routine in favor of several part-time jobs. Specialists with a core talent may choose a 100 percent freelance status. "This brings incredible strengths as well as significant challenges," King says. Experts can be added to support a new venture without a permanent financial commitment. When employees work remotely, there is also a savings in office space and overhead. "On the other hand," King notes, "many organizations have not considered best practices for managing a team that is either partially or completely virtual. Learning how to capitalize on a new, more fluid work style can be very economical. There are a lot of ways that you can twist this Rubik's Cube and discover powerful solutions for managing workflow."

Morphing from a hierarchy with the CEO at the top to a network with the CEO as the hub makes for a different approach to leadership. "My company is entirely virtual," says King. "Some employees are in the Twin Cities, where I live, but others are in Wisconsin or New Jersey. We are location agnostic, and our clients are all over the United States. There's no water cooler or coffee maker where we stop to have a quick chat, so we are incredibly intentional about our culture. Everyone understands and is on board with the mission that

I'm setting for the organization and for client work. Excellent communication skills are fundamental.

"My role is not to micromanage," King notes. "It's up to me to open space for my team. I am the buffer and the problem solver. I protect them so that they can feel safe and motivated to bring their best work forward. Coaching is a big part of our culture. We are a learning organization. Every project is an opportunity to learn. I recruit people who complement my skills and have unique strengths. Together we create impactful solutions.

"I've cultivated a dedicated team. Our ability to be experimental and creative bonds them to each other and to the business. They realize that they are continuing to learn and that I care about their development. Those elements are incredibly important. We are able to do our best work together in an environment that is entirely computer mediated."

In the midst of relentless technical evolution, one constant remains. Member experience continues to be the core association value proposition. "Some organizations understand that better than others," says King. "It's a conversation we need to elevate. Customization is currently a huge market driver, and the idea that associations can provide an experience that is unavailable elsewhere is imprinted in their DNA. Now, the challenge is to understand segmentation so we can create experiences that resonate.

"One of the images I often include in my presentations is a family-sized Snuggie. It's big enough to cover mom, dad, the kids, and the RV," says King. "I use it to make the point that so many of our education offerings are designed for everyone, but learning is not one-size-fits-all."

In her book, *Competitive Advantage: Create Continuing Education That Is Profitable, Sustainable and Impactful*, King states, "Producing a program for everyone is the same as producing a program for no one. If learners cannot identify themselves and their needs in your program, they will find a more compatible option." Designing education with target audiences in mind results in the powerful *this is for me* response that drives sales and participation. The future success of associations depends on abandoning vanilla. Learning experiences must become variegated, tailor-made, and transformational enough to create butterflies.

Topics for Group Discussion

Are you making assumptions about your association's status in the marketplace?

- If so, what ideas could you abandon?
- How could you improve market scanning?

Do you make a practice of testing ideas in the marketplace?

- Do you act on that feedback?

Are virtual teams in your organization's future?

- Have you studied how to manage and lead remote employees and teams?

Do you know enough about your members to offer customized education and products?

- If not, how could you begin to gather this information?

Meet InspirEd

InspirEd develops reliably profitable, sustainable, and impactful continuing education to advance workforces. The company is location agnostic, with headquarters in Minneapolis, Minnesota. It serves clients with a talented (and fun!) seven-person team that is still growing.

Get to Know Tracy

- **My favorite people**—Are authentic, curious, and a little sassy, and love to laugh.
- **My most memorable meal**—So many! My favorite meal right now is short rib udon with a side of kimchi at Masu Sushi & Robata here in Minneapolis. It's so tasty and comforting. It's become a happy place where the waitstaff know my name.
- **I've always wanted to**—Go on one of those Van Gogh biking tours in Europe to see landscapes he painted and enjoy French wine and cheese on pit stops.
- **I'll never forget**—The look of pride on my dad's face when I told him I was writing a book and had a publisher.

CHAPTER 9: HOSTUTLER

THE OPPORTUNISTIC ENTREPRENEUR

Kevin Hostutler, President, CEO, and Co-Founder, ACGI Software

> *"We don't need giant personalities to transform companies. We need leaders who build not their own egos but the institutions they run."—Susan Cain*

You can make almost anything with LEGO bricks, from a replica of the Taj Mahal to a life-size giraffe. But Kevin Hostutler might be the first person to use them to build a culture. Hostutler, who is president, CEO, and co-founder of ACGI Software, developed a unique staff appreciation and recognition program around LEGO minifigures. That creative application of an unusual medium characterizes Hostutler's approach to business.

ACGI develops and delivers innovative software to help associations, credentialing organizations, and association management companies (AMCs) change the world.

Hostutler's fondness for LEGO probably has to do with the fact that he's a classically trained engineer. "For me, being an engineer shapes my perspective," he says. "I'm a problem solver. I love to build things that people use every day.

"I'm a big fan of the STEM curriculum (science, technology, engineering, and mathematics)," states Hostutler, "but I use very little of it in my day-to-day work. The skill I do call on frequently is critical thinking. When I graduated from college in 1990, I imagined that I would be using my engineering degree to create 'stuff' like bridges and airplanes. But I ended up working for a company that built software for professional associations. I did that for nearly seven years, and it became my passion. I grew up on big project implementations for some well-known organizations. We developed systems for everything from membership and subscription management to accounting and other core applications."

A technological disruption catapulted Hostutler from his comfortable life as an employee into the risky but exciting world of entrepreneurship. "In the early to mid-1990s, the transition to client/server computing or networked PCs began," he recalls. "Microsoft revolutionized the software industry, and I was laid off. Although the firm that I worked for was one of the leading providers of association software, when the company saw the investment in resources and time that was needed to switch to the new technology, they decided to stop production.

"On Friday the 13th of September 1996, a day I'll never forget, my co-workers and I were called into a conference room and handed pink slips," recalls Hostutler. "My wife was expecting our third child in three years. The hardest thing I had to do was go home and tell her that I had no practical means to support our family. Even though

I knew it wasn't my fault, I remember thinking that this is what failure feels like. That didn't last long.

"The next week my customers started calling. My business partner, Dan Kasprow, and I had been working on some large project implementations. Those clients hadn't gone live yet, and they needed our help.

"One customer had a partially built membership renewal customization. All the organization's cash flow was riding on bringing in those dollars by the end of the year, and they were desperate for us to complete the job. That association was just one of many organizations that had been abandoned by the company and were begging us for help.

"Necessity is the mother of invention. It took Dan and me eight business days to incorporate. A week later we were open for business. Dan was a bachelor, and we were working at his dining room table. Needless to say, that didn't last long. With our first check we bought two laptops, and we rented an office. I began my career with a great job in a company I loved until they kicked me out of the nest. Twenty-three years later, ACGI Software is thriving and many of the customers who needed us back then are still with us today."

Be Bold

"Eventually, because I'm an engineer, I wanted to build software, so we moved from consulting and supporting a platform that was no longer viable to building a product of our own," Hostutler says. "That was an important juncture in the company's development. It was 1997 and we made, what was for us, a significant choice. We decided to skip over the popular client server technology and produce a web-based platform. At the time this was quite a leap. There wasn't a lot of infrastructure to support migration to the web. Most people weren't even quite sure what the internet meant.

"Before we began building a new product based on internet technologies, Dan, who is an even bigger nerd than I am, did the research. He discovered that we could be the 27th vendor in our marketplace with a client server platform or the first with a web-based product. Of course, being the first had a lot more appeal."

This bold move, like the partners' decision to start the company, was also partially driven by necessity. "It was 1998, and one of our customers wanted us to build an application that would tell members in real time exactly where classroom spots were available for them to take a certification course," says Hostutler. "The goal was for members to be able to quickly reserve a place at the most convenient location. The process had previously been done by fax, and registrants waited hours, or sometimes even days, to learn whether they had secured one of the limited seats.

"Delivering on this client's request gave us the confidence that a web-based application could be a broadly used tool. It was an early implementation of the software as a service concept, and it was a fun problem for us to solve."

Stay Customer Focused

As confident as Hostutler and Kasprow were about their decision to jump a rung on the technology ladder, the strategy was fraught with risk. They worried that they had outrun their toolbox and that technological invention wouldn't happen fast enough to allow them to mature, stabilize, and develop the infrastructure to make web-based applications a sustainable platform for delivery. Fortunately, innovation and technology stayed several clicks ahead of their business. However, getting an association community, known to be skeptical of shiny new toys, to come along at the same pace was more concerning. Once again, their customers were integral to their success.

"We started a company because our current clients needed a solution to bail them out," says Hostutler. "That is the DNA on which our business is built. To educate the association world about this new platform, we contacted our customers who were running our former employer's legacy software and explained the benefits of converting. We knew their data structure, and we were able to get them up and running fairly quickly. Our customers invested in our success, and that's really how we got our start. We were, and continue to be, customer focused."

Push the Envelope

To grow both as a business leader and a person, Hostutler, who is a voracious reader, looks to some of his favorite authors. "I saw Jim Collins present on his book *Good to Great* at a digitalNow conference in the early 2000s," he says. "That motivated me enough to read his books. Patrick Lencioni, who wrote *The Five Dysfunctions of a Team: A Leadership Fable,* was also a digitalNow presenter and is an author I admire. Susan Cain's book, *Quiet: The Power of Introverts in a World That Can't Stop Talking,* is another title that made an impact on me. Both as an introvert and an engineer, it was fascinating to learn the science that goes on in the brain to shape personality. John Harbaugh, head coach of the Baltimore Ravens, is also a leader I admire. I've read the stories on how he motivates the team, and I love the concepts, many of which have nothing to do with football. Reading has a big influence on my behavior and on how I manage my business. I'm driven by the desire to continually improve.

"One thing I've learned is that you've got to push the envelope. Associations struggle with that more than other types of business. I think they are caught up in the idea of preserving what they have, and they don't want to rock the boat. In the early 2000s, many organizations thought they were going to lose market share in the education arena to the dot-coms. That fear motivated some groups to successfully transform themselves.

"Associations have a rich history of providing for their constituents. They must tack away from the fear of change, have the courage to leverage their position of trust, and take their members where they need to go. This will become increasingly urgent as the workforce grows younger. I have five children. Three are out of college, and I'm watching how they approach their jobs. They look at employment very differently than my generation."

Provide Voice and Meaning

In addition to his children, Hostutler's new hires have also given him a vision of how the younger generation is changing the workforce. "We recently brought on a group of user experience (UX) designers and user interface (UI) engineers. They have tremendous energy and enthusiasm, and they love working together and doing peer programming. As an example of their ingenuity, I asked one young woman how she went about learning new technology. She told me that she studies at night in her free time. She belongs to an online learning community, and she was excited about technology that I knew nothing about. Just the night before, she had submitted a project for public review, and she was eagerly anticipating feedback from people all over the world to improve her skills.

"As employees, this generation of workers is looking for more than a paycheck. We hired our UX/UI team from big companies, such as Verizon and MedStar, where they were unhappy because they didn't have a voice or a sense of purpose. ACGI's mission to help our customers change the world resonates with them. They want to make a difference. That idea has a lot of appeal to me, too."

Strengthen Culture

Hostutler looks to changes in his own use of technology to predict future business models. "Last Christmas I bought an Alexa for our household. My four boys and I talk sports day and night. Those conversations typically ended with my son DJ looking up the answer to some esoteric question on his phone. Now we just say, 'Hey Alexa, who won the world series in 2004?' Watching how our interaction with that little device has increased over the last year has been eye-opening. My kids are growing up asking Alexa questions that we would have had to research and google. She doesn't always give the right answer, but it's hilarious to see them struggle with how to frame the request correctly. And, each time we ask her something, Alexa gets a little better at understanding the nuances.

"To me, the future of associations has to involve access to information and knowledge for members that is intuitive and voice-based. Associations should be able to easily provide answers to questions like: How many CE [continuing education] credits do I have? How many more do I need for certification? What courses are near me in the next few months? That all must be standard operating procedure."

Hostutler sees building a culture of innovation as central to keeping pace with technology. "I'm passionate about shaping our culture," he says. "Recently, to get everyone thinking creatively, we added a Shark Tank component to our company meetings. It gives any employee with an idea a platform to present their innovation. The concepts can range from technology tools to work environment and process improvement, but the request must be specific. The goal is to get one or more executives to sponsor the initiative. We work with submitters on their pitches to help them consolidate their thoughts, articulate their proposition, and have the courage to defend their idea in front of the entire company.

"One of the first projects we supported was to build an Alexa integration into the database. The group asked for $50 for equipment (to buy an Echo Dot, a speaker that connects to Alexa) and three people for two days to do a hackathon. Plus, they wanted pizza delivered for dinner. We requested specificity and got it! It was fabulous to see them pitch their idea and field the feedback from peers and executives. A successful two-day hackathon and four pizzas later, that feature is an important part of our product line and our strategy for an improved user experience.

"A second culture booster involved implementing PropFuel, a great tool for individual and team recognition. Staff are able to give 'props' (a digital high-five) to each other that the entire company can celebrate. We average twenty-plus props per week. My favorite is the dancing hamster emoji. PropFuel also provides a feedback forum involving both survey questions as well as discussion topics with responses that are visible only to me.

"The survey questions are a nice way to get to know the staff and what they are passionate about. They can be silly, such as, 'Who is your favorite superhero?' or 'What is on your binge watch list?' The discussion questions, on the other hand, provide a pipeline for feedback on how we are doing as a company. They could include topics such as, 'What are our core values?' or 'Which of our five missions this year has you most excited and why?' This tool creates a consistent opportunity to discuss what is and is not working."

The third culture booster Hostutler initiated revolves around his desire to reward performance and his fondness for LEGO. "I never announced this as an official program, but I started writing employees thank you cards to recognize their good work. As a bonus, I included a LEGO minifigure to represent their achievement. If you crush your service delivery goals, you might get a LEGO with a cowboy hat because you cowboy'd up! If you're the top performer in your group, your LEGO minifigure will be wearing a top hat. Our

UX/UI team each got a little mini chef because they're cooking up good things and hitting their roadmap milestones.

"People have started stacking the LEGOs on their desks," says Hostutler. "It's a playful way to thank employees for doing a task that might otherwise go unnoticed. Those small acknowledgments keep a culture from slipping into negativity and reinforce appreciation and gratitude. In the first 18 months of this program, I handwrote over 400 thank you notes and distributed nearly 600 LEGO minifigures.

"These days, if I'm feeling a little down, I shop for LEGO accessories. Yes, I'm not embarrassed to say that I accessorize my LEGOs. From machetes and megaphones to brooms and wrenches, they all have a very specific meaning and purpose. I have just one rule when it comes to our staff recognition program; there are no gratuitous LEGOs, no exceptions. Each one MUST be earned. Watching the LEGO figures accumulate sends a message to the entire team that we value individual effort, we take pride in group accomplishments, and we have many people on whom we can depend to move us in the right direction for the future."

Topics for Group Discussion

Is your organization in the habit of thinking boldly?

- If not, what could stimulate a more audacious approach to problem-solving?

Are your members/customers investing in your success?

- How could you leverage member loyalty to move the association forward?

Is fear a factor in your decision-making process?

- If yes, how can you mitigate fear and make deliberations more objectively?

Does your organization give employees voice and purpose?

- If not, what could you be doing to provide a more meaningful experience for your team?

Is your organization providing members with an intuitive interface to information and knowledge?

- How far are you from integrating voice-based response into your customer service activities?

Meet ACGI

ACGI Software's® mission is simple—develop and deliver innovative software to help associations, credentialing organizations, and AMCs change the world.

ACGI's two products—Association Anywhere® association management system and Certelligence™ credentialing management system—help professional and trade associations, credentialing organizations, and AMCs to achieve higher levels of performance by enabling greater efficiency and agility, which in turn generates higher revenues and smarter growth.

Get to Know Kevin

- **My favorite people**—Coleen, my beautiful bride of 28 years. My best friend from college, Fr. Dave Pivonka, TOR (a Catholic priest) who is now the president of our alma mater (so proud).
- **My most memorable mea**l—Any Thanksgiving Day meal. Deep fried turkey and a smoked turkey breast with all the

traditional sides and my entire family around the table to share it with.

- **I've always wanted to**—See my Cleveland Indians win a World Series, attend a European Ryder Cup where the USA actually wins (Rome 2022???), be in the Baltimore Ravens draft war room on draft day.
- **I'll never forget**—Walking my one and only daughter (my princess) down the aisle on her wedding day.

CHAPTER 10: ROBINSON

STRIKE THE BALANCE: SEEK PERFECTION, INSPIRE VISION

Kim Robinson, CAE, President, FrontlineCo

"Greatness and nearsightedness are incompatible. Meaningful achievement depends on lifting one's sights and pushing toward the horizon."
—Daniel H. Pink

Kim Robinson vividly remembers her first day as an independent business owner. She was alone in her office unpacking a new computer and printer when the magnitude of the change she was about to experience hit. "I came from a Cabinet-level position in government. I had a department of people working under me and an entire information technology team for support. I remember thinking—wow, this will be a whole new world. I realized that as an entrepreneur I would need to focus on the big picture, but I was also about to learn lots of tasks that weren't previously in my skill set."

Starting out, Robinson only had herself to manage. So, she was able to gradually build the foundation for a thriving company. That was in 2002; as of 2019, FrontlineCo has grown to a staff of sixteen. From health care and nursing to trade associations and women's organizations, the company's professional approach to association management has earned it both awards and clients across the industry spectrum.

Keep Finding Opportunities

"A lot of people think that entrepreneurs are serial business owners," says Robinson. "I've only launched one company. For me, entrepreneurship means taking a visionary approach and never being satisfied with the status quo. To survive and be successful, you must serve your clients and your members, and you should also be scanning the horizon to identify new developments. I don't want to be the biggest association management company [AMC] in the country, but I aspire to be one of the best. Nothing stays the same. To survive, you've always got to be looking for the next opportunity to improve service."

With a degree in political science, Robinson began her career in state government. "I loved government. There are so many good things about that work for a young person. You have the opportunity to assume significant responsibility, accomplish great things, and make an impact at an early age. My career began in public relations. Gradually, I took on larger roles, and eventually, I was managing departments. After almost twenty years, I worked my way up to a cabinet-level appointment. It was a terrific job that fulfilled many of my career goals, but those positions aren't permanent."

Not seeing interesting challenges on the horizon, Robinson cast her sights in another direction. "I always knew I wanted to start my own company," she says. "I had understanding and perspective about government, but I wasn't sure where those skills would lead. Because I believe in coalition building and had facilitated a variety of collaborations and partnerships in my career, I had worked with many associations, and I knew people in the community."

When one of Robinson's contacts was searching to recruit an association manager, Robinson happily accepted the position, and her new business was born. "There are many parallels between government and associations," she explains. "Both sectors prioritize mission rather than profit. The chance to take my skills in this different and exciting direction was what attracted me to the association world."

Word got out about Robinson's business, and she quickly had more than one client. "Initially, I believed that I could execute across several organizations," she recalls. "But I began to realize how much work is involved in running even a small association, and I knew that the staff would need to grow along with the business."

Be Efficient to Become Creative

To keep matching growth with performance, Robinson focuses on efficiency. "There are so many critical tasks that are also repetitive," she says. "My vision is to perform those essential services perfectly and to commit to implementation processes that are highly efficient. When a member goes online to pay dues, the experience should be seamless. The ability to complete routine jobs quickly and easily frees time for more creative work."

To inspire innovation at FrontlineCo, Robinson looks to her colleagues and beyond to the great minds in business. "I read so many business books and publications," she notes. "Daniel Pink and

Guy Kawasaki are two of my favorite authors. Both have motivated people across multiple industries. .orgCommunity and ASAE [American Society of Association Executives] are organizations that have also exposed me to original thinkers. .orgCommunity's entrepreneurial orientation is unique in the association space. It's an organization that looks outside our sector and puts members on a bigger playing field. That's what I try to do in my own life."

Robinson's passion to explore new perspectives and fresh insights will be central to success for all association leaders both now and in the near future. "This sector is undergoing a major transition," Robinson notes. "The universe has changed significantly in the last ten to twenty years. We are in the middle of a generational shift, and nobody has completely figured out how the new demographics will affect membership organizations.

"I have clients that are more than one hundred years old, and what's obvious is that we can't keep repeating what we have done for a century. Even though the uncertainty is stressful, the opportunity to help an organization discover innovative approaches is exhilarating. The benefits extend beyond me and my own business. Sharing insights with others in the industry and learning from our collective experiences improves the landscape for everyone.

"I believe that the entrepreneurs, who are driven to find solutions and solve problems, are going to provide strategies for success in this new environment. It's an Amazon world. Our members are Amazon customers, and that experience becomes the baseline."

Public affairs is an area Robinson views as important to the future and in which she often shares special expertise that associations may not have previously explored. "Advocacy is a catchall term that means different things to different people. In my experience, most association leaders do not fully understand the arena. I've worked hard to explain what can happen if you don't pay attention to how your industry is treated in the public sector," she advises. "Politics and government are a whole different world that will continue to be significant for membership organizations. I've tried to make it more accessible."

Build a Framework for Success

Collaboration is a thread that runs through Robinson's career. So, it's not surprising that as a leader she values a team approach. "Our company is small, but it's not a strict hierarchy. We have the most fun and are truly productive when we are together brainstorming. That's the best part of having my own business. The staff is relatively young, and they're all great workers. But there's a balance to be struck between giving people the freedom to use their talents and providing a framework and guidance so that they truly can work independently.

"As a group, we have a high bar. Everyone is expected to pull their weight. It's an environment where people sort themselves out. We are focused on service and putting the customer first. Those are the values that we live by. People who need careful supervision and a strict hierarchy are probably not a good fit for FrontlineCo.

"I think our work environment speaks for itself," says Robinson. "We are very progressive about providing great technology and access to training. We've just started a wellness program for our employees. I want the staff to have a sense of satisfaction that goes beyond the job and to know that we're going to support them. We're not everyone's ideal workplace, but I would say we hit the mark 90 percent of the time."

Seek Partners With Similar Values

Robinson views client relationships as an extension of her company's culture. "The biggest mistakes I've made in business involved taking on clients that weren't a good fit for the organization. In the beginning, I thought that we had the skills to manage any situation, even when the red flags were apparent. I learned that what matters most is an effective partnership with the client. The board and the staff must be a team, and both groups must approach that collaboration honestly. I am extremely careful about financial management, and I believe in being very transparent about those issues. I can't work with partners or boards who don't operate with the same level of candor. I've learned that talent is not always enough; there are issues you can't manage around.

"Today, all my contracts have opt-out clauses both for the client and for FrontlineCo. I don't believe in forcing a marriage. If you can tell early on that the relationship is not working, in my experience, it's best to step away. In those situations, my top priority is protecting my employees and the culture they've created. People are attracted to an organization because of its values and principles. When you don't live up to those, it takes a toll on everybody."

To adapt and thrive through a period of transformation, Robinson believes that associations will need to build the same kind of strong partnership she seeks in her client relationships. "Employees and boards need to communicate clearly and honestly," Robinson advises. "The associations that will be successful are carefully monitoring the rest of the business world and modifying strategies to keep pace. The board must understand, accept, and support that forward momentum."

In addition to being partners in change, boards need to move away from mundane decision-making and into a broader perspective. "It's tempting for boards to drill down to minutiae," Robinson notes. "Problem-solving is easy. The challenge is to develop a clear and consistent vision for the future. Many boards struggle to see the view from 30,000 feet. Even if there is consensus, it's difficult to maintain continuity if each incoming president has a different set of priorities. To me, a big part of the challenge is sustaining a vision over time.

Although staff aren't generally involved in picking the leaders, they can promote the concept that changing officers does not mean changing direction every year."

Adapt to Diversity

Continuity may also prove to be an issue in the future for employers. "We haven't had people that go to work for a company and stay there for their entire career in a long time," says Robinson. "Employees want a lot of different experiences. This desire for control over your own life mirrors the entrepreneurial spirit. There will be many more permanent freelancers or people who have one-person or two-person shops. It's appealing to have ownership over what you do and who you work for. I see this trend continuing for a long time."

Successful associations will adapt and support this new world of work. They'll identify how to help members who are self-employed find the services and benefits, such as insurance, that they once received from an employer. "Of course, there will still be large corporations," says Robinson. "But associations are going to have to cater to a more diverse workforce.

"The dues membership model that has sustained associations for so long is now in serious jeopardy. Yes, there are for-profit companies that have sponsorship or recurring revenue opportunities. I'm not sure that there will ever be a 100 percent transition away from dues, but associations can no longer expect that people will pay automatically. At a minimum, you've got to make the case for membership over and over again. Today, people will pay if they receive value. But value must be reestablished in every member transaction.

"There is an argument to be made that people who are more visionary and entrepreneurial are also more likely to thrive in an environment in which value needs to be constantly reinforced and redefined. I'm an association management company, so I believe in that model. One of the things that AMCs do well is deploy success across multiple organizations. When a strategy works, we can immediately offer other clients a similar solution. This doesn't mean we're giving cookie cutter advice; what we are doing is leveraging the experience of others. Association management companies are uniquely positioned to offer those future-focused, crowdsourcing type solutions.

"Whether entrepreneurs are in an AMC or a stand-alone association, they are a great fit for this environment because they see the big picture," says Robinson. "That's the hardest skill set to find. Every organization needs both the doers and the visionaries. Success lies in striking the right balance between executing well in the present and creating a compelling vision for the future."

Topics for Group Discussion

Who needs to be a visionary in your organization and why?

- Are you striking the right balance between big picture thinkers and doers?
- Are there visionaries in your organization who have yet to be identified?

Does your organization routinely scan the environment for future trends?

- What strategies do you employ?
- Who is charged with this responsibility, and how do results get communicated?

Is your organization operating at peak efficiency?

- If not, where is improvement needed?
- How could you begin to implement better approaches?

How well do your organization's board and staff communicate?

- Is dialogue conducted with trust and respect?
- Do both groups listen equally?
- What steps would create better understanding between the two groups?

Meet FrontlineCo

FrontlineCo helps association boards focus on their mission and deliver outstanding service to their members, providing the expertise, insights, and energy that make board service rewarding (and fun!). This award-winning association management company has earned a reputation for delivering exceptional service to its clients. FrontlineCo has a proven track record of helping clients develop top-notch continuing education programs, host outstanding conferences, leverage technology to improve member experience, and effectively represent their members before legislators and regulators. The company serves small to medium sized association and works with their boards to fully execute their vision.

Get to Know Kim

- **My favorite people**—Beyond my family, my favorite people are those with positive energy who love their work. I'm fortunate to have a lot of those in my life, especially my coworkers and clients.
- **My most memorable meal**—A few months before my mom passed away unexpectedly, I was driving home from a meeting and still had a two-hour drive ahead of me. I decided to drop in to see her and my dad anyway. We had a great impromptu dinner and talk. It was one of the last meals we

shared before she died. It's a good reminder to take those opportunities when you have them.

- **I've always wanted to**—Build a business that would be challenging and fulfilling, with a great team around me, and serving great clients who view us as partners.
- **I'll never forget**—The decision to hire my first employee. I knew I was accepting the responsibility for someone else's well-being. It was a big leap at the time, but now as I hire my sixteenth employee, it has gotten a little easier.

CHAPTER 11: KNECHT

LEVERAGING OPPORTUNITY FROM INSPIRATION TO ROI

Joseph (Joey) Knecht, CEO, Managing Director, Proteus.co

"Your Immutable Laws are the solid, healthy root system that will grow giant, mongo pumpkins every time. Dare to be exactly who you are. Let your business be an amplification of your authentic self, and watch it grow by leaps and bounds."—Mike Michalowicz

Proteus.co, Joey Knecht's company, is aptly named. In Greek mythology, Proteus.co was a god of rivers and oceans. Like his domain, the water, he was a shape-shifter. He also could foretell the future. Prescience and the ability to adapt and leverage new opportunities as they surface are qualities that are integral to Knecht's personality and his approach to business.

"I grew up in a family with a tremendous work ethic," says Knecht. "From an early age, I understood that you have to hustle to make a dollar. My grandfather was a successful entrepreneur who, in addition to operating one of the largest construction companies in New York City, also owned many restaurants. He started out poor and, later in life, despite losing everything, remained a very jolly man. My father was a police officer, and my mother was an administrator in the local public schools. Our family believed, and still does, that if we work hard the opportunity to do great things will come our way. The reality is that in the United States, you can do whatever you want."

Knecht joined Proteus.co as an intern in 2001. Although he's been with the company for 21 years, his role has been one of constant change. The first product Knecht worked on, a tool to move files between Mac and PC platforms, is a measure of how far the business has evolved. "We solved a problem that was critical at the time," says Knecht. "When I joined Proteus.co that product had twenty-one resellers. We built that number to 400 by the time the internet killed it."

Discover Growth in Problems

The company's next move was into product development. "We became a resource for corporations in the area of process refinement and productization—what's popularly called creative/design thinking," Knecht says. "I've built over 200 enterprise products and solutions. All of those inventions were born from a client's systemic problem or a tremendous opportunity that was based on that challenge. We became very successful at creating technology products for others. So, my next initiative was to develop software that allowed us to do that more rapidly. Instead of charging an hourly fee, we were able to switch to value-based pricing, which increased our profitability substantially. In addition to Proteus.co, we now own seven other technology-based SaaS [software as a service] companies."

Knecht's company is based on helping others resolve their most demanding business conundrums, and he moves seamlessly from one challenge to the next. "The deliverable might be a piece of software or something else," Knecht notes. "Not every issue holds an opportunity. Although the best solution may not lend itself to commercialization, the process of identifying a problem, analyzing it, and finding the top three bleeding points is at the heart of being an entrepreneur.

"I think entrepreneurship is misclassified as the purview of the young," Knecht says. "I see it as a mind-set. We are always looking for the next place to make an impact. Entrepreneurs grow by solving new puzzles instead of being satisfied with their progress. When you embrace the idea that you own the success or failure of your invention, it is empowering. That excitement is lacking from many people's lives. They don't feel as though they have control over their jobs." Knecht lives this philosophy and strives to instill it in his team. All the employees at Proteus.co own 15 percent of the parent enterprise and all invested ventures. "Everyone who works here has a stake in making the company better. I think it's addictive for people to have that opportunity."

Validate First

Building a network of satisfied clients has been instrumental in helping Knecht expand his business. People began coming to him with problems to solve and ideas for new enterprises. "We invested products as well as capital and provided ancillary support. At one point our venture capital company, VentureTech, included thirteen or fourteen different businesses.

"Today, our newest product, ProteusEngage, is doing extremely well. To develop it, I followed the same strategy I've used with all my other projects. I began by interviewing about 120 CEOs and vice presidents of sales at companies with $10 million to just less than $1 billion in revenue. Each executive was asked to identify their top three pain points. I said, 'I don't care if you tell me you can't find good garbage cans. I will make the world's best mid-market garbage can manufacturing company known to man.' They chuckled, but the joke served as an introduction to discuss their real problems. I learned that many were struggling with their qualified-to-close sales process. We developed a hypothesis around that concept. We were able to presell hundreds of thousands of dollars' worth of product on contracts and letters of intent; this process drives adoption and validation. So, we already had cash flow guaranteed before the product was even created.

"Validation is a big reason to sell before you build," Knecht advises. "Our success is high because we identify critical issues. Although the technology and business culture have evolved, I've used the same systematic approach with every product—validate an idea, then take it to market and do it swiftly. Within at least three months, you need to be able to have what I call the 'no go' meeting with your leadership team. There should be substantial backing before you proceed to the next level."

Knecht cautions against letting personal bias influence the evaluation process. "People get drunk on what is personally engaging for a variety of reasons. They might be passionate about the product, love the idea, or imagine that it could get them involved with the right people. There are many variables that prompt leaders to invest in products that aren't a valid or sustainable business. It's important to assess the market capitalization you're trying to create. The approach to building a nice $5 million company is completely different than the process to create a company that you can sell for $50 million. You need to know which path is right for you."

Build a Reservoir of Ideas

Entrepreneurs grow their inspiration from seeds planted in the past as well as current experiences. "I was lucky to have two important mentors early in my career," Knecht recalls. "Drs. Don Nelson and Muhlin Chen, the co-founders of our firm, have both been influential. Dr. Nelson was the person who recruited me. He received a PhD from Stanford and co-founded the Computer Science Department at the University of Nebraska-Lincoln. Although they were both academics, they believed that learning needs to blend theory, research, and real industry problems. I've always thought that was a valuable way of looking at innovation.

"They taught me to learn from each product that we build. Every new venture is a system of rinse and repeat. We identify the things that went well or were difficult and then we apply that knowledge to the next project. Having very candid partners and clients has helped us along the way. Many of my clients have been with us for twenty years. A colleague I haven't talked to for a decade might call me one morning at 7 o'clock to brainstorm a project or an issue. I've built a network of trusted folks who bring me opportunities or challenges. Each in their own way has navigated my personal journey."

Knecht believes that humility is the key to getting people's best ideas. "I was talking with our team and client success senior leader, Jessica McMullen, about building our client success model for a new product, and I observed that the willingness to learn from others and to be frank about what we don't know is one of our strengths. When we interviewed business leaders about our new product and service model, we didn't approach them with a solution or even tell them that I understood the problem. We honestly wanted to hear their challenges. I reasoned that the best way we could build a world-class customer success model is to interview executives at companies where we know they are doing it right. We needed to honor their accomplishments and ask for advice. That transparency is a strong technique that opens people to helping you and an amazing way to learn and grow yourself and your business."

Live Your Values

Understanding his strengths and staying true to those talents keeps Knecht on track as a leader. "I know myself. I'm a hands-on innovator. I like to participate in the validation and the problem-solving. I'm also very goal oriented. Our company values are commit, create, give, grow, (C2 G2). Living those values means hiring really strong talent. Each employee needs to be competent because we are not micromanagers. We use Gino Wickman's book, *Traction: Get a Grip on Your Business*, to guide our operations. We have a five-person leadership team. Everyone is very transparent. All our activities are measurable, and we're growth oriented. Our culture and my leadership style reflect those principles.

"The company can only be successful if all legs of the business are strong—finance, sales, development, and client relations. If any area is out of balance, it's a threat to the organization. My role is to be what Wickman calls a visionary. I'm responsible for aligning the elements that are needed to see the future. It's those strategic, big picture issues that tee us up for success."

Knecht believes organizations need to exercise their culture. "We don't try to control our culture, but we feed it and reinforce it daily. Every morning we do a jump-start, and each week we discuss one of our values. We also recognize accomplishments with kudos and accolades, and we support each other's work. When someone needs help with an important project, a process called Red Dot gets put in motion."

Knecht's team makes having fun together a priority. "Our culture group arranges a company-wide lunch every Wednesday. On a larger scale, they planned an organizational trip to Mount Rushmore. We took our entire staff and their families to visit this historic site and participate in a team building hike."

The company values serve as a measure to assess new clients. "The strongest thing that a leader can do is to protect the team. If we feel that a prospect is not a healthy fit for us, we won't pursue that engagement."

Self-evaluation and feedback from colleagues are among the tools that help Knecht refine his company and his leadership skills. "I'm a member of the Entrepreneurs' Organization, and I belong to a forum of nine other people who own enterprises. We use Mike Michalowicz's book, *The Pumpkin Plan: A Simple Strategy to Grow a Remarkable Business in Any Field*, to evaluate our progress together. We even share our personal and business finances. One of Michalowicz's concepts is the importance of getting rid of the bad pumpkins that keep the best ones from thriving. Not only have these exercises helped us weed out impediments to growth, but we've actually been able to identify new products and new ways to expand our businesses."

Continue to Evolve

The idea of finding growth by pruning and culling a business model is one that can be valuable to the association community. "Membership declines when people don't believe what they are getting is worth what they are spending. The internet and other variables have broken the value chain," says Knecht.

"The phone in your pocket has 100,000 times more power than the processor that landed the moon rover. Everything has changed. When I started with the firm, our product was a cross-platforming tool. At the time that model was valid. When it became obsolete, we moved on to the next problem. We reviewed our clients' needs and studied their bleeding points to discover how we could build on our strengths and continue to serve. It's a process of evaluation and evolution. Success isn't just a matter of whether people need your product, it extends to how you deliver, price, and support what you sell.

"Overhauling those systems means reinventing the company. You can do it incrementally or make hard shifts. But to me, it is the essence of entrepreneurship. My father-in-law is a farmer. There is substantial disruption going on in agriculture. Every industry has these challenges. But people adapt their strategies to the market. Maybe if an association has 50 employees today, its future iteration will have 15 or 300. If you are providing value under your charter you shouldn't be bound by present norms. You must think about how to gear up for the next fifteen to twenty years because that planning has to begin now.

"Leaders need to recognize the importance of investing in the future," states Knecht. "They should be putting capital into activities that will be relevant in the next ten years. As an example of how rapidly technology changes business, we recently built an online management platform product for an association. Their board was convinced that everyone would not be buying online and that they would still need a thirty-person call center. Last year, 99.5 percent of their business was online. The call center was reduced from thirty people to four employees. It's a much more successful organization, and the members are getting more value. Nonprofit or association doesn't mean that it's not a business, and you need to operate accordingly."

Relationship and network building have always been a primary driver of association membership. "It is a mistake to imagine that people need to be members or that just because someone belongs to a profession, they will join the affiliated association. I have friends in financial services. There are multiple associations in that arena. My colleagues really struggle with deciding where to invest their professional development dollars. Technology is eroding the value of face-to-face networking. My philosophy is that the conference model is dying. People want to network and learn on their own time and when the need arises. One of the strongest values of the Entrepreneurs' Organization is the fact that I have access to a database of every member/business owner in the world. If I'm in Dallas, Texas, next week I can have a coffee with a colleague and continue to grow."

Build Incentives to Win

Lack of a vested interest in success can stifle an association's growth. "Associations don't have owners," Knecht notes. "There is a charter, and there are many transient people. If the organization is failing, the CEO must be the person who mobilizes others to put the business back on track. However, an executive director on a standard two-year contract has little motivation to take the risks required to move the organization forward. Incentives can help to support and encourage that decisive action.

"In addition to inspiration and the drive to succeed, a great CEO has to be a salesperson at heart. They need to approach operations from a product orientation," says Knecht. "Leaders must understand how to leverage technology and minimize politics in their organizations. I think a lot of people are tired of the politics that pervades many associations. They see that 2 percent of the membership are driving the bus and the other 98 percent are along for the ride. Executives need to find ways to make participation more equitable and enjoyable."

Be Courageous

Courage unlocks the ability to adapt to the future. There is no learning without failure. "As a child, I was taught that I wasn't always going to win," Knecht advises. "When you fall, you get up, try again, and do it better the next time. The United States is a country where, with hard work and a good idea, you can be whatever you want. I've always been passionate about that. Don't be afraid to grow big pumpkins. Throw your heart into cultivating your best ideas, and ruthlessly weed out the tired strategies, sacred cows, and unquestioned habits that are holding you back."

Topics for Group Discussion

What challenges in your organization could also offer the seeds for growth?

- Would a systematic approach to identifying those opportunities be beneficial?

How skillful is your organization at adapting to changing business realities?

- What has changed in your business environment that your association has yet to address?
- What are the consequences of inertia?
- If you believe you are adapting successfully, what are your strengths?
- If you are not successfully adapting, what is holding you back?

Do you approach business questions with humility?

- Do you regularly seek broad-based advice and information?
- What external groups or people could provide valuable input in your decision-making processes?

How could an association "presell" products?

- What are some effective strategies for evaluating success before bringing a product to market?

Meet Proteus.co

Proteus.co is the result of the VentureTech (formerly i2rd) and Vipa Solutions merger in 2017, founded in 1993 by Dr. Don Nelson and Dr. Muhlin Chen, professors from the University of Nebraska-Lincoln's Computer Science Department. Both men recognized the need for software development to be a collaborative experience with a mix of business, technical, and feedback from end users to ensure success. Over the years technology has changed, but the founders' core principles and values hold true today at Proteus.co. Year after year, Proteus.co's clients have valued the company's honesty and integrity. They have trusted Proteus.co to deliver best-in-class products, and together the company and clients have developed long-term relationships for business success.

Get to Know Joey

- **My favorite people**—My wife, Jennifer Knecht. We are true partners. My parents, Ed and Kathy Knecht. My mentors, a ton of them.
- **My most memorable meals—**
  Coaching—A retired IBM exec talked about hustle and how you need to create your opportunities.

Business dinner—In Japan shared dinner with Eric Clapton and his team.
Business dinner—The countless number of meals that I asked for candid feedback and I did receive. These truly grew us/me.
Personal—My wedding.
Relationship—My wife and I did a dinner with leading experts in relationship management and understood how to support and grow each other.

- **I've always wanted to**—Be better than I was yesterday.
- **I'll never forget**—September 11, 2001. Promises made to loved ones. To solve Problems.

CHAPTER 12: JUDY

TO GET WHERE YOU WANT TO GO, KNOW WHO YOU ARE

Charlie Judy, Founder, WorkXO

"Determine what behaviors and beliefs you value as a company, and have everyone live true to them. These behaviors and beliefs should be so essential to your core, that you don't even think of it as culture."—Brittany Forsyth

Charlie Judy's career has taken him from the buttoned-down world of suits and corporate conference rooms to the gritty thrill of growing a business from inspiration to market. Across that continuum, people have been front and center in Judy's imagination.

"I spent more than 22 years as an executive in large to mid-size enterprises," Judy recalls. "I was a human resources [HR] professional, a certified public accountant, and a client advisor. During all of it, I loved—more than anything—working really closely with my team to simply-engineer HR...to make it less complex and more accessible, to make it more about the human and less about the resource, and to build a community."

That community's success is Judy's passion. He was chief human resources officer at Baker Tilly, one of the largest public accounting firms in the country, when he realized that he needed to follow another path. WorkXO, the company that Judy and his partners Maddie Grant and Jamie Notter built, was founded with the vision of helping organizations intentionally manage their workforce experience and the culture that fuels it. QuestionPro, a global survey-based analytics company, bought WorkXO in 2018 and Charlie now runs their Workforce product line.

"I have always been fascinated by the intersection of people and data," says Judy. "Fifty percent of HR professionals say they rarely, if ever, do anything meaningful with their employee surveys. Yet, analytics are increasingly important, if not imperative. Although we're getting better at getting data, we're not necessarily getting better at making it relevant. I thought that was a problem that our team could solve."

Gather the Right Data

Judy and his partners set out to build a model that uses information to improve culture. "We wanted to give organizations meaningful data about the workplace in a way that drives actionable results." The entrepreneur's stock-in-trade—research, validation, and revision of their idea, took the team in unexpected directions. "What we found," said Judy, "was that organizations wanted better information about their employees' actual experience at work.

"With that goal in mind, we developed a survey platform focused on understanding culture. The instrument was designed to objectively uncover behaviors that exist or do not exist in an organization. It doesn't measure whether or not the culture is healthy or encourage suppositions about what makes a great workplace. The questions are designed to produce raw materials that organizations can use to improve decision-making and sharpen focus."

Notter and Grant's familiarity with the association industry meant that the partners' early work began with that community. "Jamie and Maddie had established relationships with many association leaders. So, when we launched a pre-technology prototype in 2016, associations were a natural focus," Judy notes.

"We discovered that they were thinking seriously about their work environments and were hungry for information. There was a strong desire for transformation in operations, administration, and environment. Understanding culture is foundational to that growth. You need to explore the behavior that is holding you back and identify what must change. Knowing who you are today helps you become much smarter about who you need to be."

A personal epiphany sparked the idea that is central to WorkXO's approach. "My 'aha' moment came when after 22 years I realized that my sense of connection, purpose, and passion about any job had less to do with the company than with how that organization got work done," Judy advises. "I realized that I've been employed by many organizations lauded as 'great places to work,' but they weren't always great for me. The salary, benefits, and perks, like free lunch or flextime, might be perfect for someone else. But if I was missing a set of behaviors that fuel my fire, I don't care if the company has made every list of the best places to work in the world. It will not provide an environment in which I can be successful.

"Organizations need to achieve that level of clarity. You have to understand the characteristics of work in your culture. That specific information allows employers to hire people who are the right fit for their community, and it can help prospective employees avoid situations where they will not thrive. For example, if being a decision-maker is a non-negotiable for you and you're considering a job where decisions are only made by committees, then I don't care how much you like the breakroom, the people on your team, or your career path, you will not do your best work. That's a simplified example, but it's the kind of idea that woke me up."

These are the core concepts that informed WorkXO's original vision. Judy and his colleagues realized that to deliver their message they would need to package it in a way that was efficient and appealing to their audience. "Even before I partnered with Jamie and Maddie, I knew that to differentiate in the marketplace, we would need to productize the solution. In today's world, innovating is often enmeshed with technology, like it or not.

"However, the technology is secondary," Judy advises. "It's the bun for the hamburger—a delivery system. We were confident in our understanding of the market and in the model that we built, but we're not technologists." To create the electronic framework, the group turned to software developer, Joey Knecht at Proteus.co. "Joey and his team did something unique. Of course, they developed the architecture and wrote the code for the platform, but they also helped us verify that we were building the right product."

Know When to Get Help

"So often entrepreneurs make the mistake of having a great idea, whether it's a technology or a new donut, and they build it without completing the due diligence needed to successfully launch," notes Judy. "There's a methodology to entering the entrepreneurial environment, and we needed a Sherpa to guide us through that terrain. Joey and his team were really good at keeping us from falling off a cliff.

"With any new business or product, it's important to understand when outside expertise is essential to get to that next level. In my work with associations, I often encounter the urge to create new products," Judy says. "It's understandable, given all the data and information at their disposal. But 90 percent of the time people aren't aware of the process that needs to occur before a successful rollout.

"A firm like Proteus.co can walk you through that maze. They'll test the market to ensure that you've built the right mousetrap, evaluate the audience, and determine how much those customers are willing to pay. There is a whole community of people who are experienced in developing products and taking them to market. A lot of us have learned the hard way. The willingness to realize when you are wrong and that you cannot have all the answers is a core competency."

Timing is another of those critical skills that is part intuition and part experience. "The firms that I admire the most," Judy explains, "are those entrepreneurial giants who are good at taking the first step. They know their product isn't as shiny, flashy, or pretty as it will be one day, but they're willing to let people start kicking the tires and to discover what customers think. The goal of this experimentation is to bring you closer to your vision—to arrive at a better iteration of the model. That was the hardest thing for me to learn. Entrepreneurs aren't afraid of mistakes. You have to be very comfortable with hearing no. Negative feedback doesn't mean that you have the wrong product. It provides an opportunity to adjust and to keep moving closer to the ideal.

"I have learned this from working with software development companies. Sometimes you need to roll out a technology that isn't

100 percent baked because you want to see how it works in a real environment."

Focus Inward/Scan Outward

Judy's experience as a business owner has changed the way he views leadership. "I came from an environment where I had a team of 35 people who were all capable and trustworthy. My role was to position them to succeed. In hindsight, that's easy. What's harder is figuring out how to lead with limited resources—to make the right investment at the right time in the right place. I realize now that I need to get out of the way and allow people to use their skills.

"In a high-growth start-up—limited resources, accelerated timelines, big expectations, and a tremendous load of deliverables—there is a low tolerance for mediocre talent. You must have the right people in the right seats, and you need to be very selective," advises Judy. "If you hire the wrong employees at the least it's lost opportunity and at the most it's failure. I'd like to think that I'm getting better at putting the best people on the team.

"As a leader, balancing attention between your business and the market is also important. One of the things that we measure in our cultural assessments," says Judy, "is how good organizations are at getting an outside perspective on what is happening internally. What people want today is old news. The trick is to determine what customers will ask for next. Being entrepreneurial means predicting people's needs 12 months or three or even five years from now.

"You must always have an ear to the ground listening to your constituents, paying attention to the signals they are sending and assimilating those variables into your strategy. That wide lens is reflected in the advent of open-source technology. People used to be very proprietary with software and coding. Now the outlook is that many eyes and hands are likely to make the product better than it otherwise would have been."

Define Outcomes

One of the characteristics of a successful organization is a common vocabulary with language that everyone understands in the same way. "For example," Judy says, "when a group decides that they want to be more entrepreneurial, each person attaches their own meaning to that term. Typically, we don't acknowledge that this is not a switch we can flip. There is a journey to take. The first step is to define what the goal means to us as a group: What does success look like? What does it feel like? What does it sound like? Then we must assess who we are today and what behaviors and systems need to change to bridge that gap. Having a town hall meeting and saying that you want to focus on innovation is not enough. You've got to go deeper and arrive at an organizational awareness about the desired result."

Judy sees the traditional corporate structure as one of the biggest impediments to taking the plunge into cultural understanding. "We are still rooted in the idea that people at the top make the decisions. But that's not how the world works today. The command and control structure is ingrained in our DNA. It's really the hardest thing for traditional organizations to break through.

"Entrepreneurial groups can dispense with the outdated model. It shouldn't matter what my title is or how long I've been with the organization," Judy notes. "Whoever is closest to the problem gets to fix it. If you recommend a strategy that is better, stronger, or faster, we're not even going to have a meeting about it. We're going to run with your idea because you're in the best position to make that decision. That's challenging for even the most innovative organizations. A board of directors makes this kind of flexibility even more difficult. Associations need to be realistic about whether they can create a nimble environment."

Foster Collaboration

Collaboration, partnership, and knowledge sharing are characteristics that Judy believes will contribute to the association community's future success. "We need to make outside experts an integral part of our organizations, even if they don't have the same logo or the same email address. Leaders should borrow from the open source perspective and consider pooling resources. Third parties bring a fresh approach to the conversation. It's important to stop being insular and to instead cultivate an open attitude. Be willing to put heads together."

A more collaborative workplace will welcome and necessitate different types of talent. "I think we're going to see a lot of fluidity," Judy says. "The traditional idea that 99 percent of the workforce are full-time employees is no longer realistic. The most effective associations will leverage human resources by combining full-time, part-time, contingent, and contractual third-party relationships to deepen the pool of expertise. Even the biggest organizations are figuring that out."

Judy sees diversity in the way people work being paralleled by a more employee-centered attitude. "Today, we are empowered to customize pretty much everything else in our lives. Our economy is very much rooted in choice. Why don't we allow for that in the workplace? If I were going to place the bet in Vegas that I think has the biggest payoff, it would be that organizations that can create a career experience customized to the individual are going to be the real winners.

"The idea that the employer holds all the cards is changing," Judy notes. "We're moving toward a less black and white world. We're going to see a shift to the other end of the continuum. For decades the customer has come first. The most futuristic view is to put the employee first." While Judy acknowledges that customer satisfaction drives success, he notes that employees are the people who have the greatest impact on that equation.

"If organizations are not shaping work around the needs, interests, aspirations, and motivations of the employee, at the least you're seeing suboptimization, and at the worst, you may be seeing disaster. Saying my employees come first doesn't mean my customers aren't important. But my customers won't increase their spend with me unless I've got the right people."

To accommodate this dynamic, CEOs will need to recognize that they are not there necessarily to run the company. Their job is to supply the vision and to pay attention in a more interactive and hands-on way to what their constituents are experiencing. "We put too much pressure on CEOs to be everything to all people. The entire staff needs to own the culture," says Judy. "CEOs should see themselves participating in that experience, not standing somewhere above it. They have data at their disposal to understand the gap between where the organization is and where it needs to be. The next step is using that information to deliberately shape the future."

Topics for Group Discussion

What behavior occurs in your organization that advances productivity and success?

What behavior hinders progress?

- How could your organization change that behavior?

Has your organization adopted any characteristics of the open-source concept?

- Would becoming more collaborative be beneficial to your organization?
- If so, with whom could you collaborate or partner?

What does the idea of creating a work experience customized to the employee mean to you?

- Is this something that would be beneficial for your organization?

Do you agree with the idea that employees should come first?

- If yes, why?
- If no, why not?
- How high a priority are employees in your organization?
- Are the people in some positions valued more highly than others?

Meet WorkXO

In 2018, QuestionPro acquired the innovative culture management firm, WorkXO, to strengthen its commitment to developing an integrated set of workplace, workforce, and people analytics solutions. The result is the Workforce product line that includes a set culture, engagement, and employee experience tools that organizations use to identify, understand, act on, and monitor desired workplace behaviors and outcomes across the entire employee journey—from recruitment to exit.

Get to Know Charlie

- **My favorite people**—My children bring me the most joy. Some of my favorite people are the ordinary men and women out there who simply make the world go 'round; those people who contribute in ways most will never know (or appreciate) and are just fine with it being that way.

- **My most memorable meal**—The night before I left Brussels, Belgium, after a year-and-a-half assignment, I took four of my best friends from my time there to Comme Chez Soi. It is a beautiful haute French cuisine restaurant with close to 100 years of history behind it and one of the best wine cellars in Europe (which we of course tasted and toured). At the time it was run by star chef Pierre Wynants, a hero of mine, and holder of three Michelin stars from 1979 to 2006. It was a fitting goodbye to my formative experience as an expat.
- **I've always wanted to**—Live on a working farm.
- **I'll never forget**—When, in 1982, the St. Louis Cardinals won the first of several World Series championships during my lifetime.

CHAPTER 13: CARUSO

GETTING TO WOW

David Caruso, Co-Founder and President, HighRoad Solutions

"There is no plan B for passion."—Chris Gardner

For David Caruso, getting the "wow" from a happy customer is lightning in a bottle. "There's a lot of joy that comes from being an innovator," he says. "My biggest satisfaction is the reaction and response from the people we serve. Customers can become emotional when you solve a problem that's causing stress. That gratitude is priceless." As co-founder and president of HighRoad Solutions, Caruso has been helping people get to wow with business marketing and automation platforms since 2005. But he still remembers the first time he amazed a client.

Coming out of college, Caruso worked for Sprint and a variety of other businesses. During that period, he also discovered associations, an unusual hybrid that was a new riff on his previous retail and commercial customers. One of Caruso's association prospects had a monthly newsletter that the organization was unsuccessfully trying to convert from direct mail to a weekly publication. "A light bulb went off in my head," says Caruso. "I knew I could find a faster, more deliberate way to solve that problem and that there would be plenty of other takers." Caruso identified a company that was doing fax broadcasting and got a job there. "We signed up 200 associations in the first year," he says. "And when the customer who started that adventure saw his newsletter rolling out of the fax machine, the first thing he said was, '*Wow.*'"

A network of close friends and a strong family are Caruso's support system both in business and in life. Ron McGrath, co-founder and chief executive officer at HighRoad, has been a colleague and close personal friend for more than 20 years. He's Caruso's sounding board for inspiration, ideas, and practical advice. The humble leaders who accomplish greatness, such as Warren Buffett and Chris Gardner, the latter of whom rose from foster care and homelessness to found his own brokerage firm, also capture Caruso's admiration.

Seek Common Values and Diverse Skills

As a leader, Caruso is more polo shirt than French cuff. His affable personality translates to a relaxed approach that easily mobilizes a diverse team to action. "My style is a little bit loose," he says. "I like to lead by example. I work with a team of smart people who can figure things out. One of my favorite quotes is by George S. Patton: 'Never tell people how to do things. Tell them what to do and they will surprise you with their ingenuity.'

"I'm not going to win one of those MacArthur genius grants, but I am someone who can get a group together and really make things happen. I have so many accomplished teammates that I've worked with over the years." Caruso's knack for rallying people across generations and backgrounds to solve a challenge is a talent that has helped HighRoad grow. "I've always been a good diplomat, no matter how diverse the group I've been involved with," he says. "That's just part of the job of leadership."

Early in his career, Caruso realized the need to welcome new generations of employees into the company and the benefits of a variegated team. "You learn that things don't stay the same. I try to maintain a staff that is similar when it comes to core values such as work ethic and lifestyle balance, but wide-ranging in skills, experience, and personality. It's important to include some self-starters, those people who just love to get the job done."

HighRoad's diversity is both human and geographic. The company's address is a post office box in Ashburn, Virginia. There is no headquarters. "One of the best decisions Ron and I ever made was to run a virtual company," Caruso explains. "Our employees live in Atlanta, Pittsburgh, Chicago, Washington, D.C., and other locations. It wasn't our plan to be virtual, but initially, we were a bootstrap business with zero revenues, which meant that our employees had to work from home.

"Today, we are able to hire the best people for the job, no matter where they live, and technology allows us to bring them together seamlessly. When you have the right team, you don't worry about distractions. I know that our employees don't need an office or a manager looking over their shoulder to be productive."

In 2005, when HighRoad was one of the few virtual businesses, the concept raised some eyebrows. "Today, the idea is more mainstream," Caruso notes. "Over time people have come to value the advantages of working at home. Businesses and even a few associations are moving away from bricks and mortar. There is no commute, and you have more time for family. I use the mornings to work out, and in the evening, instead of spending an hour on the road, I can spend the time watching my kids play sports.

"Some employees miss the social aspects of the workplace. We've tried to compensate for the lack of coffee machine/breakroom conversations in several ways. We schedule daily conference calls around a number of activities. A monthly mystery lunch is one of our most popular events. DoorDash delivers a surprise meal to the entire team, and we all sit down and eat together. I thought it was silly at first, but everyone likes it. Events like that help keep people engaged and enthusiastic."

Get Better at What Works

Learning how to create an effective virtual workspace is the result of years of experience. Practice has also taught Caruso and his partner McGrath to pick and choose their path to growth carefully. Caruso credits the balance of skills between the two with keeping the company on an even keel. "Ron's an engineer. He's a very logical, focused individual. I'm a salesman. I'm always looking over the horizon for the next product to promote.

"In about 2006, I began thinking that text messaging would be the wave of the future. I had already successfully piggybacked on the fax; I was trying to get ahead of the curve. We started by offering several different services to see which would stick. But the bottom line was, I think we made one deal in three years. Failing like that was a little heartbreaking for a new entrepreneur. It taught me that you've got to recognize what works and make that better. We put a lot of time, effort, and blood, sweat, and tears into trying to launch that platform. We learned that even though we think a product is cool, if others don't want it, we need to let go.

"Having the discipline to stop something that doesn't work is hard. When you've had some success, you start thinking that you have all the answers. It's an emotional response. Luckily Ron and I are very well balanced. I do the things that Ron doesn't like to do, and he does the things that I don't enjoy. Ron's very skilled at focusing on what the data is telling us. If the numbers don't make sense, we move on. We've learned to focus on our strengths and to identify the best clients for us. That's how we've rolled for the last fourteen years."

Helping their clients use cutting-edge marketing tools to better target, segment, and automate communications is HighRoad's current focus. "Associations have had challenges with the idea of marketing beyond their memberships and finding new audiences. Marketing automation provides that opportunity. It's been a new venture for us. Some groups aren't ready to take the leap to automation, but others already understand how these systems can help them to work more strategically."

Find Innovators

Self-starters and innovators can empower associations to adapt more quickly to marketing automation and other growth-oriented strategies. Caruso believes that an entrepreneurial approach can move associations beyond tradition. "Engaging individuals in a nonprofit or an association who are seeing outside the box," he says, "is important in terms of finding new revenue and discovering what the audience wants."

But Caruso advises that changing a long-established culture can be challenging. "Introducing newer members to an older workforce is not an easy task. In addition to involving the neophytes in the organization, you also have to incorporate their ideas. New concepts may not have room to grow within a bureaucracy that's focused on politics over productivity.

"There's a need to be more free-spirited when it comes to understanding what the audience wants and acting on that to drive growth." Caruso sees a digital transformation as one way to jump-start cultural change, although sometimes new systems are not enough. He says, "Moving an organization that is stuck in another direction is a hard decision to make. I've seen whole levels of management removed and new people brought in just to change the behavior. That may do the trick. But sometimes the new hires don't recognize how big a job they have on their hands. The good news is many associations have successfully redesigned their cultures and many more probably will achieve that goal over the next few years."

Let Go of the Reins

Younger workers are inevitable agents of change both for associations and the overall economy. "This new generation is going to drive a workforce of mobility," says Caruso. "They don't necessarily have to be in an office. They'll be working from home, from coffee shops, or from almost anyplace in the world. Diversity in experience and approach characterizes the group. The employees at HighRoad are doers, but they don't always complete the task in the way that I expected or as the job was done in the past. It's a good experience to let go of the reins and see what gets accomplished. The attitudes are fresh, and work gets done in ways that are unique to each individual."

Along with a less conventional approach to work, younger people are also bringing a more expansive concept of who fits the definition of a customer or a member. "A lot of the larger associations are starting to accept a broader audience who are not members in the traditional sense and don't have the same behaviors that members had in the past," says Caruso. "Associations will need to learn to communicate effectively with these nontraditional constituents. They will be interacting with a larger audience over time.

Technology will play a significant role in the engagement process. "One of my good friends in the industry has been working with a lot of the mid- to smaller-sized associations to help them implement virtual conferences," notes Caruso. "Finding better ways to use technology can remove some overhead and pave the way to more impactful interaction with a larger audience and improved identification of new members who fit the profile and culture for each association.

"This kind of expanded organization calls for a leader who is growth oriented and more competitive than what we have seen in the past," says Caruso. "The CEOs of the future will need to be involved, accessible, and collaborative. But the right team also feeds on the energy of the group. A good mix of diverse individuals will work collectively to find new ways of doing business and progressing over time."

Data is the focus of much of HighRoad's activity, and Caruso believes that it is also a means to future success for associations. "Associations will need to make data-driven decisions quickly in order to move forward. Fortunately, there is no business that I know of that has as much data on their clients as an association," he says. "Mining that information to provide more individualized experiences can expand the base, improve recruitment and participation, and generate revenue. Reliable data is essential to successful customer experiences, and for anyone who loves hearing 'the wow' as much as I do, data is a great tool to help you get there."

Topics for Group Discussion

How does your organization work to cultivate diversity?

- Are you diverse demographically?

- Are you also diverse in style, personality, and opinion?
- If not, what is holding you back?

If you have virtual or temporary employees, what steps do you take to help them participate in your culture?

- Do employees at your organization have enough opportunities to coalesce as a team and to socialize?
- What additional experiences could you offer?

Do you have enough self-starters and innovators on your teams?

- How do you identify people with those qualities?

Is your organization using data effectively?

- Is your association management system an effective data collection platform?
- Are you missing important information?
- How could you collect that data?

Meet HighRoad Solutions

HighRoad Solutions takes the best pre-existing email and marketing automation technology and makes it work for associations. However, reselling business-grade tools to associations just won't cut it. By building their own software and integrations on top of the same platforms that successful companies use, HighRoad gives customers the best of both worlds. HighRoad makes their own software and integrations on top of the same platforms that successful commercial companies use, HighRoad gives customers the best of both worlds. They make the world's best business marketing platforms accessible to associations

Get to Know Dave

- **My favorite people**—Anybody wearing burgundy and gold (Redskins fan).
- **My most memorable meal**—Was a blind date where I met the love of my life.
- **I've always wanted to**—Be a pilot.
- **I'll never forget**—The birth of my children.

CHAPTER 14: NAGARAJAN

DRIVEN BY PURPOSE

Amith Nagarajan, Chairman of the Board, Association Success Corporation

"For, in the end, it is impossible to have a great life unless it is a meaningful life. And it is very difficult to have a meaningful life without meaningful work."—Jim Collins

Generations of MBA students were taught that the only purpose of a corporation is to increase shareholder value. "That's a pretty empty proposition," says Amith Nagarajan.

Nagarajan's world turns on the opposite physics. As chairman of the board of Association Success Corporation, Nagarajan is a serial entrepreneur whose family of companies is conceived around the idea that purpose should drive value. "Profit is important," he notes, "but purpose is deeper and more emotionally meaningful. Purpose-driven companies strive to solve problems that impact a broad swath of people, including groups who may be outside of the typical scope of their industries."

The Association Success Corporation includes the following companies:

- **AssociationSuccess.org** is a hub for innovation and publishes original content from within and outside the association world and hosts the SURGE virtual conferences;
- **rasa.io** is a Smart Newsletter platform powered by artificial intelligence (AI);
- **PropFuel** creates email-based feedback campaigns focused on member voice and engagement; and
- **Matchbox Virtual Media** creates virtual events that seed meaningful conversations and connections.

"I invest in companies both inside and outside of the association space," says Nagarajan. "I've had a hand in about twenty different start-ups. After a dozen years of building my first business, Aptify, I felt it was important to give back to entrepreneurship and invest in businesses at the earliest possible stage. Each company is unique, but whether they are in biotech, software, or food, they are united by the common goal of advancing sustainability and growth."

Nagarajan grew up in Silicon Valley, so his passion for entrepreneurship is a nature versus nurture conundrum. We'll never know whether, as a teenager, he would have started Aptify out of his college apartment if he'd grown up in Madison, Wisconsin. "I launched Aptify back in 1993," he says. "Initially, we produced tools for all kinds of database applications. By the time we discovered associations, we had over 1,000 customers using our products. We didn't know much about the industry, but we thought that the market was interesting.

"Our roots were in high-end, enterprise technology that we developed four years before we came into the association community. Once we got involved with associations, we fell in love with the sector. We realized that these organizations are deeply committed to something meaningful and, in many cases, making a powerful impact on the world. We threw all of our eggs in one basket and said let's pursue this single market.

"This was 1997-98 and most associations were using databases that were inflexible," continues Nagarajan. "Customization was a death trap because it isolated you on the island of impossible upgrades. Aptify changed that. We introduced a platform that allowed associations to extensively configure their products, and we were successful. We had a 98 percent customer retention rate."

In March 2017, Nagarajan came to an agreement with Community Brands which he felt would offer both his customers and his team new directions for growth, and Aptify was sold. "Aptify wasn't just about making money," Nagarajan says. "It was motivated by a deeply held belief that we could significantly impact the association profession and ultimately improve society and the world through our work. I'm proud of what we accomplished as a team and the way we served clients and upheld our values. Growing a company globally is a challenge and a privilege, particularly when the work you are doing can affect so many people in different fields."

Narrow Priorities/Nurture Culture

Entrepreneurs are typically voracious consumers of ideas, and Nagarajan is no exception. "I've been influenced by many different people," he says. "When I'm asked what business books I like to read, the person I immediately point to is Jim Collins. His books, *Good to Great: Why Some Companies Make the Leap...and Others Don't*, *Built to Last: Successful Habits of Visionary Companies*, and *Great by Choice*, have been formative for me. I love the objectivity that comes from his research-based approach. I've thought through many of the concepts in his books over time and used them in a number of companies.

"Verne Harnish, the author of *Mastering the Rockefeller Habits: What You Must Do to Increase the Value of Your Growing Firm* and *Scaling Up: How a Few Companies Make It...and Why the Rest Don't*, is another writer I admire. Both Harnish and Collins recommend executing relentlessly around a narrow set of priorities while building a strong culture. Verne is someone I've gotten to know over time. He's a fantastic leader and a great teacher. Advice he gave me inspired the name for Association Success. He recommends 'owning' a word that has significant meaning in your marketplace. Because my goal is to make associations more successful, I picked the name Association Success for my family of companies."

In addition to collecting ideas, Nagarajan likes to immerse himself in the most difficult puzzles he can find. "I enjoy being involved in challenges that people imagine are impossible to solve. Back in the 1990s nobody thought you could have an association management system that was both easy to modify and to upgrade. Aptify proved them wrong and reinvented the way a lot of things were done in the industry.

"rasa.io is another example of a solution for a significant industry roadblock. Many organizations struggle with keeping their brand in front of members on a regular basis. They're good at stand-alone events such as conferences, but they haven't identified practical strategies for daily engagement. rasa.io offers a means for frequent, highly personalized interactions with members via Smart Newsletters powered by AI. It also eliminates the massive amounts of manual labor that would normally be involved in sending every recipient a customized product that is curated to their special interests. We've used some cutting-edge AI techniques to make that possible, but it's an incredibly simple idea.

"One of the lessons I learned at Aptify," continues Nagarajan, "is that when you're trying to solve a huge, time-consuming problem, it's best to start with the easy answers. So, with rasa.io our first application is the simplest one we could think of that would produce meaningful value and be easy to implement That's the kind of project that interests me—tackling a really tough issue in a way that fundamentally changes the game.

"Peter Diamandis is another influencer of mine who is interested in this type of problem-solving. His book *Abundance: The Future Is Better Than You Think*, describes how the same exponential growth that is happening in information technology is occurring in other fields, without widespread public knowledge. For example, the price/performance ratio of solar cells has halved every 16 months for the last thirty years. But most people aren't aware that solar is becoming extremely cheap. If you continue the exponential curve in this category, ten to twenty years from now solar power will be incredibly inexpensive. What will that mean for the energy industry? Diamandis's book was written in 2013. But when you look back at it five or six years later, his predictions are dead on. My point is that you try to find an exponential curve that's hidden in a field of linear thinking, and that's an opportunity that becomes exciting."

Grow People

As much as Nagarajan enjoys investing in opportunities, he relishes developing people more. "When you grow people, the by-product is that you grow your business. That's really where the fun is," he says. "Your purpose statement and core values become the foundational layers of culture. They provide an agreed-upon set of behaviors. For example, the core purpose of rasa.io is 'To Better Inform the World.' All of the company's decisions are made based on this fundamental rationale about why we exist. The core values team members are aligned around are:

- Own it
- Learn by doing
- Measure it
- Tell it like it is
- Celebrate success
- Simpler is better
- Demand diversity in thought

"These principles guide us toward establishing that long-term ideology that Jim Collins talks about," says Nagarajan. "My job as a leader is to find great people who are deeply passionate about our purpose and values and to help them grow.

"When you put people first, they pay you ten times the dividends you would have gotten if you were only thinking about the business. The goal is to grow the business as a by-product of growing our people, not the other way around.

"At Aptify we encouraged everyone to write a three-year vision for themselves; we called it a Personal Painted Picture. That exercise is foreign to most organizations. We motivated people to think outside their role, their department, and even outside Aptify."

Take Customers to a Better Place

The commitment that Nagarajan feels to his employees' growth also reflects the way he views his relationships with customers. "Too often, companies are happy to get business and they want to please their clients by providing the requested service without pushing the client in a way that could create growth. For example, it's easy to modify software to perpetuate an antiquated process a client is demanding to retain, as opposed to identifying a more effective way to work. I believe that entrepreneurs in the association community, and all markets, have an obligation to help clients realize better outcomes. You have to ask yourself whether you have achieved something significant and sustainable.

"The association management system market is one that's evolved in a tremendous way over the last twenty years. The entrepreneurs that are in this space have been able to change the way associations do business. As a group, entrepreneurs bring new ideas, opportunities, and a level of energy that associations may not have internally. We can be a fresh set of eyes."

Put a Toe in the Water

Associations, Nagarajan believes, can benefit from adopting the kind of growth-centered orientation that comes more naturally to business owners. "I've frequently been asked to speak about AI in the last couple of years. The most common questions center around how to get started with this new technology. I tell people that the first step is to fuse the idea of experimentation and growth into their culture. The problem is that association staff often worry about failure more than anything else. They're afraid that if they try something new and it doesn't work, they'll get fired, looked down upon, or suffer some other kind of career damage. That perspective is holding associations back.

"Association leaders are smart enough to do this work. They have the necessary resources too. The issue is not ability. The invisible barrier is fear of dipping a toe in the water. What I recommend," advises Nagarajan, "is picking a simple project with the idea that the only goal is to learn. Put a chatbot on your website and see what happens. Implement an AI newsletter and see how it performs. Pick something simple that you can do quickly and learn from. Don't spend six months debating what to do with the board and volunteers. Just test and evaluate.

"In order to move forward, the organization has to acknowledge that it is stuck and that inertia is preventing progress. That's a theme I talk about in my own book, *The Open Garden Organization: A Blueprint for Associations in the Digital Age*. Another book that addresses this topic is *Loonshots: How to Nurture the Crazy Ideas That Win Wars, Cure Diseases, and Transform Industries*, by Safi Bahcall.

"Bahcall discusses strategies for fostering innovation and creativity in an environment that has a legacy business model. He has a PhD in physics and a background in biotech. He looks at the issue through that lens and considers how the lessons of the natural world can be applied to organizational behavior. One of his key takeaways is that there are soldiers and artisans in every organization. The soldiers' job is to stay on the established path. They execute orders and protect what Bahcall calls the franchise business. The soldiers think that artisans are a bunch of crazy people whose value is questionable at best.

"The artisans are the creatives," continues Nagarajan. "They are the innovators whose job is to paint a picture of the future. But they're also responsible for the behavior of the current organization. It's difficult for them to build new things because they're bound by past behavior. The dilemma is separating those two activities. Plenty of organizations handle this by creating labs or think tanks. But those departments can't operate in isolation. Bahcall's book describes how to build a structure that encourages the right behavior from the best qualified people and stimulates the interchange of ideas between the two groups."

Focus on Improvement

In Nagarajan's view, the only way to stay relevant is to keep moving forward. "I was recently at a marketing conference where I heard someone say, 'You're not likely to be replaced by AI. But you are likely to be replaced by someone who knows how to use AI.' If your job is to cut down trees and you're using a handsaw, you know what happens when the person with the chainsaw comes along. If you're afraid of the new tool, that's a problem.

"Artificial intelligence right now has several narrow categories that work extremely well. The scope is rapidly getting wider and wider. We all need to be adapting personally—taking on that growth mind-set. You have to ask yourself how you can use new tools to be more productive and work smarter. Pick up a book, watch a webinar, take a course. Do something to educate yourself even if it's in a small way. There is momentum in running. I think the future is bright. But associations and their staffs need to consider how they can keep building new skills.

"I see the association model changing for the best," says Nagarajan. "Membership will no longer be the focus of activities. Things like purpose, content, and the buyer journey—issues the corporate world has been talking about for some time—will be increasingly important. Association leaders will need to look far beyond the boundaries of tradition. They'll need to understand their core reason for being—what makes them best in class and deliver on that promise.

"Finding where your value truly lies and taking that potential as far as it will go is a simple strategy for success. When you are truly driven by purpose you align naturally with the growth mind-set that is needed to keep pace with the future. Placing the highest value and priority on your purpose will never steer you in the wrong direction."

Topics for Group Discussion

Has your organization identified its core purpose?

- Are you setting narrow priorities and executing around that purpose?
- What steps could you take to discover where your greatest value as an organization lies?

Does your organization operate with a growth mind-set?

- If yes, what activities validate that response?
- If no, what steps could you take to develop a more growth-oriented culture?

Do you have the right balance of soldiers to artisans on your teams?

- How do you keep the groups separate enough to allow each to do their job?
- Does information flow between the two groups?
- If not, how could you enhance communication?

How are your teams building skills to use future technology?

- Are you able to launch experimental/learning projects?
- If not, what barriers need to be removed?

Meet Association Success

Association Success is a family of companies united by purpose. It exists to help associations achieve sustainable long-term growth, thereby significantly advancing their missions. Associations are a critical part of society and by helping them thrive Association Success is making its mark on the world. The Association Success family members are either wholly owned subsidiaries or companies to which Association Success has provided growth equity. The goal is to grow the family by adding new companies where needs exist.

Get to Know Amith

- **My favorite people**—Are folks who are willing to do things nobody else thought was possible and have the grit and determination to make it happen—across any field, whether in business, science, arts, sports, whatever. I'm always inspired by stories of people overcoming seemingly impossible odds with a sharp mind, a view towards growth, and relentless execution.
- **My most memorable meal**—In the late 1990s when I was building my first software company, I visited a customer in Tokyo, Japan. One evening after we finished up for the day, the executives from the customer took me out to a tiny underground tempura kitchen where the chef cooked up some of the most delicious food I've ever had. The experience was just as great as the food—being in a place that was clearly off the beaten path and the tourist radar, getting to enjoy a wonderful meal with some great people.
- **I've always wanted to**—Learn how to kite surf.
- **I'll never forget**—The feeling when I first witnessed an end-user working with software that I had helped write. Being able to see people use a product I had conceived of and worked hard to build was an incredibly rewarding experience.

CHAPTER 15: JORDAN

DESIGNING DIFFERENTLY

Garth Jordan, MBA, CSM, CSPO, CDT;

Senior Vice President, Corporate Strategy;

Healthcare Financial Management Association

"People ignore design that ignores people."—Frank Chimero

We all know a few lucky people who were born with a vocation. Garth Jordan didn't find his passion quite so easily. "I'm an accidental tourist," he says. Experimentation, curiosity, and his work within the association community eventually revealed where Jordan's true enthusiasm lies. He is that unique person who constantly seeks excellence beyond the status quo. "My passion revolves around risk-taking and challenging," Jordan explains. "I'm compelled to reverse any complacency within associations. I want to challenge leaders to think differently, to use technology in innovative ways, to reconsider our business model, and to lead with a fresh perspective on everything from product lines to member service."

Jordan, who is currently vice president, corporate strategy at the Healthcare Financial Management Association (HFMA), cut his professional teeth in business development. When a colleague recruited him to head a team at an association, he didn't have any background in the industry. By the time he landed the COO job at EDUCAUSE, he'd added marketing, member services, conferences, and a solid understanding of how associations operate to his resume.

EDUCAUSE, a community of information technology leaders in higher education, was a good fit for Jordan's iconoclastic spirit. "It's the most entrepreneurial association in my experience," he notes. "I was involved in some exciting cultural and facilities developments. We moved the office from Boulder to Louisville, Colorado, created one of the early open plan work environments, and developed a slew of successful new products and services along the way. Jordan's current role as a chief strategist continues to draw on his strength as a rule-breaker and an innovator.

"When I began my career, I was constantly building things that didn't exist before. Whether it was creating a new department, restructuring membership initiatives, or developing products, I was challenging the typical association's view on risk," Jordan recalls. "But even when I was responsible for major revenue streams, I rarely focused on the numbers. I was seeking opportunity. I was confident that if I delivered value by creating the experiences members and business partners wanted, the dollars would follow."

Start a Journey

"A lot has changed over the last ten to fifteen years," Jordan observes. Associations are still among the more risk averse industries, a luxury we can no longer afford. Fingertip content, education, and unique digital community experiences are eating away at our primary business model. Leaders are beginning to realize that tradition offers no safety."

When Jordan was hired at HFMA, the 38,000-plus member organization was facing challenges. The association serves financial professionals and providers who work in healthcare settings. The industry was chaotic, with mergers and downsizing, and membership recruitment and renewals were mature and nearing the top of the dangerous slide.

"The world was moving in a different direction than we were," Jordan says. There was no shortage of products and services, but HFMA's offerings weren't curated for their consumers. Members were looking for ease of access and a bespoke experience, like those offered by Netflix, Audible, and Spotify. Instead, they were getting an electronic mega mall chockablock with merchandise, complicated pricing structures, and gordian navigation. The association's business model was stuck in 2010 while their customers were looking for a 2025 approach.

Design thinking was the catalyst that allowed HFMA to explore the future through a new lens. This problem-solving methodology has only recently emerged on the association horizon. It centers around developing a deep, empathetic understanding of the organization's constituents and, through a process of experimentation and iteration, building what they want and need. Adapting design thinking as the framework for their strategic planning process, Jordan and his team launched the organization on a multiyear journey of radical transformation. There were no sacred cows; membership, business models, product lines, organizational structure, and technology platforms were all up for review.

The HFMA began with their endgame in mind. Their goal was to become the Netflix of associations. Like the entertainment giant, the organization wanted to make it easy for members to access all the content they need for success, in the formats they enjoy, for a competitive price. "We believe this will help us do a better job of supporting our members to create a sustainable future for healthcare in the United States," says Jordan.

"After multiple rounds of research and loops in the design process, our solution modeled on the successful Netflix formula emerged." Jordan explains, "You can access us on any platform—whether you are in your home office, on your phone at Starbucks, or searching your tablet during a meeting—it doesn't matter. Members can view one webinar, become certified, contribute to our online community, or utilize our entire experience portfolio for an all-inclusive price. We're also watching the statistics carefully to ensure that the content we roll out is relevant.

"When we launched the all-inclusive price in November 2018," notes Jordan, "it was a 24 percent increase over the previous cost. We were nervous—even with all the research backing our decision. But renewals increased almost immediately. Seven months later, we launched the fully integrated digital platform, which will enable scalable growth into new markets. Now, when I search on a keyword, I can retrieve and access the related information across the entire organization, from community content to videos, podcasts, online learning, certifications, and more. Then, I can filter the results based on what is most useful. It's a very contemporary experience."

Early statistics indicate that HFMA made the right decisions. Renewals have maintained a 7 percent increase on average week-over-week. The number of new members remains consistent, and HFMA will be launching a planned recruitment campaign pointed at both market penetration and expansion. "Our new targeted groups are likely to be more loyal than in the past," says Jordan. "Because the new digital experience includes built-in analytics, we now have real behavioral data to show us what people are consuming in the overall portfolio and where we need to adjust. These analytics give us a holistic view of model performance, so that we can become a more focused learning organization.

"Netflix uses behavioral data to invest in developing their original content, diversify their programming, and create customer loyalty. Their platform allows for constant redesign and experimentation, and we're heading in the same direction!"

Be Brave

It takes courage to rock the boat, to be someone who is willing to champion a difficult project based on the strength of the outcome. Jordan found inspiration early in his career. "Dr. Diana Oblinger, the CEO I worked under at EDUCAUSE, was a tremendous role model for me," Jordan recalls. "She had an open and engaging relationship with the board and with me personally. She believed in experimentation and encouraged me to search for the next best thing for the organization. Her willingness to let me play in the sandbox allowed me to be daring and challenge the status quo. Diana created a culture in which the entire staff was receptive to the idea that the present is not defined by the past.

"John Brockman is another person who influences the way I think. He is a literary agent and innovator whose organization, Edge.org, explores significant issues from a variety of perspectives. Brockman asks great thinkers of our era the same big question and summarizes their opinions. His book *This Explains Everything: Deep, Beautiful, and Elegant Theories of How the World Works*, outlines elegant, simple reasoning for many thorny topics. It's helped me to consider how we make much of our work in associations more complicated than it should be. That book is the inspiration for my mantra, 'Start with simple.'"

It doesn't matter how innovative or right you are if others won't buy in to your plan, however. Design Thinking, the process that HFMA uses in its organizational transformation, is a strategy that promotes collaboration. Initially, the focus is on exploring the human side of the issue. Qualitative data and research about people's behavior in related situations are collected. Jordan elaborates, "As a designer and an entrepreneur, starting from the customer perspective develops empathy. People can see that you already understand them and their relationship to the problem. They realize that you distilled their input into unique, meaningful insights that identify the specific challenge that needs to be solved, and they feel included even when they may not have participated in all the previous conversations."

Winning over a board on a hot button issue can turn from lively debate into an executive search quickly enough to make less confident leaders avoid the situation. Processes, such as design thinking are important, but timing is also critical to achieve consensus. Jordan didn't come by his negotiating skills without experiencing a few teachable moments. "When I was a newer COO working at the Medical Group Management Association, the CEO resigned," he recalls. "She and I had been working to restructure the organization's traditional membership model."

Jordan thought the time was right to accelerate the process. He didn't realize that the board and staff were still trying to manage the leadership change. "My reluctance to take a time-out was part personality conflict and part stubbornness. When you want to be entrepreneurial within an association, you have to assess the readiness of all the players." The right moment disappeared along with the previous CEO. Jordan let his eagerness for organizational improvement overshadow the human variables of the situation.

Build an Entrepreneurial Culture

Are one or two trailblazers enough to move an association into the future? Jordan doesn't think so. "An entrepreneurial approach is only valuable if it permeates the entire culture. You can design a new product anywhere. An association is a safe place for development because you aren't using your own money. But the payoff isn't in building things, it's in creating unique value, and today that often requires a different vision and approach; changing the business model is hard to do. In some cases, it means swimming upstream against decades of tradition.

"I want to see associations help their members become better problem solvers. That involves understanding where their real professional challenges and interests lie," says Jordan. To achieve deep knowledge and elegant solutions, the design process needs to become more empathetic, experimental, and iterative. "This is soup to nuts," he says. "True innovation requires an insightful starting line. Then, you're ready to ideate, prototype, test, analyze, and recalibrate."

Jordan views online communities as a step toward a better understanding of the member perspective. But he notes that those interactions often occur in an ad hoc fashion that doesn't lend itself to thoughtful problem-solving. Communities are an example of the heightened information sharing and collaboration that Jordan believes characterize the future workplace.

"These are trends I see amplifying. I have a daughter in college and one in high school. Their educational experiences, compared to my own of forty years ago, are vastly different. A large portion of their education is learning how to physically and digitally collaborate on complex projects. As their generation enters the economy, they will set new expectations about how humans work together. We've only scratched the surface of teamwork and problem-solving. Associations should be out in front of that trend in a big way."

Sharing and borrowing from the larger business community is a good strategy for breaking free of traditional structures. "Future leaders will need to bring a diverse background and skill set to the table," Jordan advises. Digital transformation and annuity revenue streams, as well as product development and operations, should all be within their experience. The courage and discipline to end activities that aren't productive and to focus on what the organization does best will be essential. "I often see CEOs who were hired from the industry they represent being almost completely outward facing," says Jordan. "They spend 80 percent of their time with public relations and networking, and I'm not sure that evolves the organization. If I were to summarize what diversity brings to the table, it would be someone who is a human-centered designer—who can be the architect to build a vibrant new business model that serves their members as well as Amazon does. Why should our expectations of an association leader be any different? Just because you have less money doesn't mean you can't be insightful and innovative."

Even with the right attitudes and people in place, turning a tanker around is a lot trickier than changing course in a sailboat. "Coupling innovation and associations creates an interesting dichotomy," Jordan says. "People think of entrepreneurship as fast. We talk about failing fast and learning from failure. I agree with that approach in a small business, but larger organizations need to be patient with the cyclical process. This can be challenging for board members. It's difficult to have enthusiasm for initiatives that may not begin or end on their watch. The board must understand that a big project, like HFMA's Netflix of Associations, includes many smaller entrepreneurial and operational initiatives. True innovation—the strategies that breathe growth and energy into an organization, require perseverance and a commitment to ongoing evolution."

Topics for Group Discussion

How does your organization balance the variables of customer experience versus revenue?

Is design thinking a concept that could be valuable to your organization?

How empathetic is your planning process?

- What could be done to increase the customer focus?

How do you assess members' satisfaction with their customer experience?

Is your organization's business model still viable?

- If yes, make the case.
- If no, what are the next steps?

Meet HFMA

The HFMA is the nation's premier membership organization for healthcare finance leaders. The association builds and supports coalitions with other healthcare associations and industry groups to achieve consensus on solutions for the challenges the U.S. healthcare system faces today. Working with a broad cross-section of stakeholders, HFMA identifies gaps throughout the healthcare delivery system and bridges them through the establishment and sharing of knowledge and best practices. The association helps healthcare stakeholders achieve optimal results by creating and providing education, analysis, and practical tools and solutions. The mission of HFMA is to lead the financial management of healthcare.

The organization was founded in 1946. It has assets of more than $30 million, revenue of more than $25 million, and more than 44,000 members.

Get to Know Garth

- **My favorite people**—Are those who create with purpose.
- **My most memorable meal**—Is always the last one. I'm not much for dwelling on the past, honestly.
- **I've always wanted to**—Climb all 53 mountains in Colorado over 14,000 feet. Just a few left. I'm going to have to come up with a new "I've always wanted to" statement soon!
- **I'll never forget**—Taking a huge step as a shy teenager by drawing and giving a picture to my first crush—and future wife. I realized taking risks pays off.

CHAPTER 16: WARD

PURSUING THE FREEDOM TO SHAPE THEIR FUTURE

Meg and Tim Ward, Co-Founders,

Gravitate Solutions

> *"Entrepreneurs are closer to artists than any other career. Because, while we teach art appreciation and art theory, art is experiential and it's passion driven."—*
> *Steve Blank*

If you think AWS, MongoDB, and Python sound like good names for goldfish or gibberish, you could ask technology visionaries Meg and Tim Ward to translate. These wizards of information technology (IT) believe that, "A pot of black coffee and a good idea can change the world." Their company, Gravitate Solutions, proves it daily by helping associations solve the kind of computing challenges that make you want to crawl under your desk and stay there forever.

For Meg and Tim, the freedom to shape how they contribute to the world and their work is just one of the advantages that outweigh the long hours and substantial responsibility of owning a small business. The opportunity to innovate and create is another.

"I want to be able to make my own decisions," says Tim. "The whole idea behind entrepreneurship is bringing a specific and unique value to market that people will appreciate and be eager to use. There's an enormous amount of accountability inherent in building a business. Our staff depends on us for their livelihood, and we take that incredibly seriously. Yes, there is risk, but we are driving the ship."

Follow Your Bliss

The Wards share the kind of independent spirit that drives many small business owners. "When I graduated with an engineering degree from the University of Virginia, most of the people in my class took jobs with IBM and other big companies. A corporate work style didn't feel like a good fit for me," says Tim. "I wound up being employee number one for a software start-up." Developing a new platform from ground zero was exhilarating until the moment when Microsoft unveiled Windows and left its competition, including Tim's employer, in the dust.

"That was an early lesson in innovation and disruption," Tim notes and laughs. Tim followed that experience with a stint as a management consultant for some far less mercurial employers. He counted a number of Washington, D.C., heavies among his clients, including the Executive Office of the President, Office of Management and Budget, Defense Information Systems Agency, and USAID.

"It was an interesting experience," he recalls. "But someone with an entrepreneurial attitude wants to see things happen more quickly." Tim's career took a déjà vu path and confirmed his passion for invention when he landed at Avectra, another newly established software company as, once again, its first employee.

Meg, quite literally, grew up in a family business. "My childhood home was the antique store that my parents owned. Customers were always in and out. Sometimes they would even be invited to dinner."

Meg's grandparents were also merchants. In keeping with the adventurous attitude and strong stomach needed to become independent owners, the couple opened their Maine jewelry store in 1931. It was the Great Depression, and most people were running to the pawn shop with whatever could pass for bling, not thinking about buying a new bauble. But Meg's grandparents made a successful life and set an example for their family.

"I started my career in publishing at a time when the industry was consolidating and shrinking," says Meg. "All those layoffs made an impact on me. I saw the downsizing as a result of poor management. Since we've had our own company, many of the decisions I've made have been weighed against that context. I ask myself if the direction we are taking will be both stabilizing and fruitful."

In 1999, Meg made the move to the technology sector. The speed of the IT world is exciting for both Wards, but matching it to the resources of their association clients can be a challenge. "Nonprofits crave all the bells and whistles that are available to the corporate world, but their funding and staffing may not allow that level of sophistication. Our goal is to bring clients the best solutions possible within the limits of their personnel and budgets," says Meg.

Meg and Tim began their own business journey in 2007. Tim was working at Avectra as chief technology officer. "It was a good job," he says. "But I had just turned forty years old, and we had small children. I missed working more closely with clients, and we were both strongly attracted to the freedom that being independent would bring." Avectra was an open platform for the vendor community, meaning that the software could be used and modified by other programmers without changing the source code. Gravitate Solutions was born when Meg and Tim seized this opportunity to capitalize on their knowledge of the product and passion for customer service.

History, even family history, has a habit of repeating itself. Shortly after Meg and Tim set up shop, the country plunged into a recession. Their business launched in an economic environment that was almost as rocky as the one that Meg's grandparents survived. Despite that precarious start, the Wards have never looked back.

Evolve With the Environment

"We started the business in a loft in one of our bedrooms," says Tim. "From there, we moved to a room behind a dry cleaner in Alexandria, Virginia. Then we opened an office in Springfield, Missouri. The hum of tanning beds was our soundtrack because we were located in back of a beauty salon. Eventually, we secured class B space in both locations. Now, our offices are class A and far from our humble beginnings."

As Gravitate's space has evolved, so has its workforce. "The way we attract talent and our work processes have change significantly over the last twelve to thirteen years," Tim notes. "Many of the original folks are still on the team; now they're just a smidge older. Everyone used to be in the office, and there were lots of tablecloth lunches because people didn't care if their day stretched till 8 o'clock or 9 o'clock at night. Today, many of our employees are parents and working from home four days a week.

"The changes in the workplace have made us very flexible. We find smart people who fit the culture, and we accommodate them," Tim says. "Our goal is to hire great people, give them a vision, and let them run with it. But I've kept my tech chops sharp so that I can have conversations with our engineering team, and they know that I understand their work."

Tim and Meg have found successful strategies that balance their individual leadership strengths. "We have a good yin and yang for running the business. Our skills complement each other," Tim says. "I like creating, working with teams, mentoring, and teaching. The day-to-day human relations activities are not my strength."

Meg runs the operational side of the business. "I focus on the teammates," says Meg. Everyone is different, so I adjust my management style to meet their needs. I spend time getting to know each person and learning how to motivate them and keep them happy. Sometimes when people are considering working with us, they ask what it's like to run a business as a married couple. We established early on that there can only be one boss, and the head of our team is Tim. He is the leader. This arrangement works well for us, and we're both extremely comfortable with it."

Lose the Drama and Listen

Tim credits the years he's been in business with honing his leadership skills. "The importance of being a good listener is one of the things I've learned that is not so obvious. As an engineer, I'm trained to solve problems. I've discovered I need to stifle the impulse to rush to a solution. In situations where there is disagreement, it's best to wait until everyone has had their say. If you try to force a solution, people become defensive or withdraw."

The Wards promote creativity and innovation by creating a culture of openness. "We strive for no drama and no ego," says Tim. "We encourage everyone to speak their mind and to identify what is not working. It's a good strategy for getting engagement and buy-in."

Hiring employees who are the right fit for this positive environment is a top priority. "Our interview process is rigorous," says Meg. "We do phone screening followed by three waves of interviews with teammates from different cross sections of the company. There are role playing exercises, and the final activity is a cultural fit session. We look for candidates who are willing to be flexible and have the intellectual gravitas to dig into problems that we're asked to solve every day. This process ensures that we hire the right people."

Bringing candidates who are less adventurous along on the creative journey can be challenging. "Cautious people are probably not going to be a great fit for Gravitate or many of the small businesses in the association space. If you want a safe job, the government or a big corporation is a better choice," says Meg.

Tim adds, "We do have a lot of people on staff who are engineers. I don't know if they're cautious, but they are certainly risk averse. Leading by example has been successful for us. When we were building our new product, Nucleus, I threw myself into it and led the charge right down to the code level. The same thing happened when we started our Salesforce practice; I completed the first training. I laughed at myself when I made mistakes. It helps employees push themselves when they see that the boss tried something that didn't work. I don't like to include failure as part of our culture. But I do think that there's room for trial and error. You just don't want to make the same mistake over and over again."

Although the Wards leave their employees plenty of room for experimentation, when it comes to customer service, Meg emphasizes that the approach is not negotiable. "Mistakes as we develop our processes and products are one thing. But when the client requires us to deliver, failure is not an option. Our clients trust us. If we try something that doesn't work, we absorb the cost.

"We've done a good job learning from our own experiences. We pivot when things are not working. There are no sacred cows. It could be my own great idea that we need to abandon."

Break Barriers

Tim finds significant parallels between their business and the association community. "Many of our clients are the same size we are," Tim notes. "They have comparable staffing and generate similar revenue."

"Except for possibly the twenty biggest associations, we are all small businesses," Meg agrees.

The difference is that associations have boards and bureaucracy to contend with. "It takes an entrepreneurial mind-set to break some of those barriers," says Tim. He believes that the association sector has arrived at a point at which innovation is no longer optional. "To survive, associations will need to embrace digital transformation. Apple spoiled everybody. The member expectation is that interaction will be as simple and easy as something they do on their phone. It's a struggle because organizations are resource constrained, and it's hard to keep up with change that is happening so quickly. A challenge for people like us is to help associations get to where they need to go. Competition from all kinds of other learning options and platforms makes this an exciting, pivotal time."

"Frankly, I'm a little worried," says Meg. "Our data analytics product, Nucleus, is installed at a lot of client sites, and we're seeing weakness in the new member category. We're helping clients to turn that around and to identify and concentrate on what makes them most relevant."

The ability to stay focused on value needs to start at the top. "Many people believe that associations should run more like businesses," says Tim. "The reaction to that has been to hire a CEO from the corporate sector. But future success really isn't about profit and loss. I think it depends on operating as efficiently and cleanly as possible, in other words, being entrepreneurial. Eric Ries, author of *The Lean Start-Up,* proposes a business approach that offers a lot of value for the future. His methodology is characterized by experimentation, openness to customer feedback, and product and systems design that is iterative, as opposed to static."

"CEOs need to be courageous in order to cut through the noise and execute, whether it's implementing a new program or evolving staff skill sets," says Meg.

The Wards see future association leaders operating in a rapidly changing work environment. Some human resource professionals are predicting a labor shortage as a result of Baby Boomer retirements and the small size of the generation following that large cohort. Although the talent pool may be getting shallow, it is also growing wide.

"We have employees in Michigan, Missouri, India, Ukraine, and all over the world now," says Tim. "I also think freelance specialists are going to be important. For example, we don't have a graphics person on staff, so we rely on freelancers for logo design and other similar needs. When we started out twenty-five years ago, everybody had an IT department and programmers. That's never going to come back. As associations are required to do more with fewer resources, freelancers are going to fill some of that need."

"I'm intrigued with the freelancer model coming to the fore," says Meg. "I'm curious to see how we marry that with the need for people with deep experience in certain areas. Gravitate makes an enormous investment in our talent. We take care of our people because their expertise is so important, and we want to make sure they enjoy what they do.

"In the future, people will be working from anywhere. The need to be able to use technology will be ubiquitous. I worry about kids who may not have access in elementary schools. I'm committed to addressing that inequality through philanthropy because I think it's a game changer. Some children have $400 smartphones, while others can't do their homework because they don't have access to the internet. That's a big deal."

Do Good in the World

Heart is one of the special qualities that the Wards believe distinguishes associations from other organizations. "Associations are purpose-based," says Tim. "Their activities are driven by mission and cause. That's a real advantage. Activism also resonates with the younger generation, who will be the newest members. Meg and I say our clients are trying to do good in the world. That's a wonderful place to start if you have a business."

Meg adds, "Associations are able to bring people together to share a common experience. I believe that's unique and valuable. How they leverage technology and other tools to keep that heartbeat strong, not just at the annual meeting, but throughout the year, will be central to their future success and well-being."

Topics for Group Discussion

How important are productivity and sustainability in your decision-making process?

- How do you evaluate whether an activity will contribute to those qualities?

How does your hiring process vet for cultural fit?

- Are the behaviors and attitudes that contribute to your organization's positive culture clearly defined?
- How are staff educated about culture, behavior, and attitude?

How does your organization ensure that employees enjoy what they do?

- Is employee fulfillment a priority?
- Is that value conveyed throughout the workplace?

Do you agree that courage is an important value for CEOs?

- What prevents CEOs from acting courageously?
- What could be done to eliminate those barriers?

Meet Gravitate Solutions

Gravitate Solutions serves member-based organizations. The company lives and breathes databases—and data—and uses tools such as Bootstrap, Power BI, and netFORUM to make the world a better place. They are masters of their crafts who are highly trained in the tools they use, because there are no shortcuts to success. The company has 50 employees and offices in Springfield, Missouri, and Alexandria, Virginia. They were ranked five consecutive years on the *Inc. Magazine* 500\5000 list of fastest-growing companies. Gravitate is the creator of Nucleus, the first data analytics product for associations.

Get to Know Meg

- **I've always wanted**—To see the Northern Lights.
- **I'll never forget**—When the Red Sox (finally!) won the World Series in 2004!
- **My favorite animal**—Is the elephant.
- **I've always wanted**—A classic VW Bug convertible.

Get to Know Tim

- **My favorite people are**—My family and my University of Virginia fraternity brothers.
- **I've always wanted to**—Be the third guitar player in the Rolling Stones.
- **I'll never forget**—My wedding day or my kids being born.
- **In my free time**—I like to swim, play guitar, and sample craft beer.

CHAPTER 17: STEVENS

A PASSION TO BE UNIQUE

Dan Stevens, President, AssociationTV®/WorkerBee.TV

"You don't have a real strategy if it doesn't pass two tests: First, what you're planning to do really matters to enough customers; and second, it differentiates you from your competition."— Verne Harnish

When Dan Stevens was a newly minted entrepreneur, his father wrote him a letter that changed his life. At the time the advice, which Stevens's dad called "low cost excellence," alarmed him. That parental wisdom has since become a personal mantra. "My father told me that if I was doing things the same way next year as I did them this year, I should be very nervous. That warning woke me up," Stevens says.

"Verne Harnish, an author and speaker whom I admire, says that if you want to be in business, you've got to be unique. If you're hiring people who could work for any other company and you're pricing the same as your competition, you're not different. Even in 1986, my dad was aware that to be successful you need to be a chameleon—constantly changing with the environment to avoid irrelevance or disruption."

Stevens has been refreshing his vision and his business models for most of his life. He values the freedom that being an entrepreneur gives him to be a creative problem solver. "There are so many niches in the market where there is room to invent something new." Association TV® (WorkerBee.TV's flagship video and multimedia platform and videocentric services for associations) is Stevens's second business, which he founded in 2007. The challenge he sought to overcome was that video is complex and expensive to do well. "But everyone wants access to this powerful storytelling medium. Our company has a simple value proposition," he says. "Association TV makes video profitable, purposeful and predictable. We use video strategically to tackle issues associations face and help them improve the three big R's: retention, recruitment, and revenue."

Feed Passion and Follow Principles

Owning a business gives Stevens the flexibility to feed his passions. "Ever since I graduated from university, I've traveled the world. I love learning about history and other cultures," he relates. "We have a big map in our house that chronicles our family travels. My three adult daughters now compete with me on who has the most flags representing places we have visited. They are catching up!"

Independence is a way of life for Stevens. "It's taking control of your life rather than letting others manage it for you. I work away from the office 12 to 16 weeks a year. In a few days, I'm headed to the cottage. I am fortunate to be working there for the next three weeks. I'll be doing business while traveling in Europe and Africa very soon as well. Even though I'm halfway around the world, I'm never disconnected. I answer to my families (both work and home) and to the promises we stand behind for clients. Those concepts are my guiding light, and technology allows us to serve from everywhere."

Associations play a leading role in growing Stevens's company as well as in shaping his professional development. "I was just five years into my first business when I founded the Winnipeg, Canada, chapter of the Entrepreneurs' Organization in 1991. I served five years on the international board and one year as the international chair. That peer-to-peer learning opportunity gave me perspective on so many facets of management for both associations and business. I learned about leading teams and building a vision that is inspiring to volunteers. I also had a firsthand opportunity to discover the challenges of running an association and the importance of proper synergy and distance between board and management. In the process, I made friends around the world."

Early in Stevens's relationship with the Entrepreneurs' Organization, he collected another piece of advice that is a touchstone. Family, faith, friends, fitness, and finance are what a colleague called the five F's. He cautioned that even a brilliant multitasker can't give equal time to each of those facets of life, but if any one of them gets near zero, you are in dangerous territory. This concept forces you to set goals, manage each area to avoid burnout and, more importantly, lead a significant life.

"At the time, I had three young children, I was International Chair of Entrepreneurs' Organization, and I was growing my own business," Stevens recalls. "This guidance helped me stay married and make time for my family when I could easily have been a workaholic. I coached my daughters' hockey and soccer teams and volunteered for my association. I still set goals and make plans in each area. If you ask my wife whether I'm in balance, she'll say, 'Absolutely not,' but I never let myself get to zero. The prioritizing I do to fill each of those buckets has shaped how I look at my life as an entrepreneur."

Don't Wait to Pivot

Technology is a foundational element in Stevens's career. "My first venture was a technology systems integration company," he notes. "We automated manufacturing and distribution systems and the supply chain from the CAD [computer-aided design] diagram through the shop floor and up the supply chain to the general ledger. When I sold that business in 2005, we had offices across Canada and a few in the United States. After the sale and a one-year stint in transition, I took a year off to decide what was next.

"During that sabbatical, a colleague in the Entrepreneurs' Organization was dabbling in video. He was enamored with the medium and saw its value as a vehicle to educate workers all over the world, hence the name WorkerBee. That enthusiasm inspired me to investigate using video as a platform for a new business. I realized that associations already had the content and the audience. My goal with WorkerBee.TV was to help them leverage and monetize assets they already owned and showcase their brands in a new context while creating a simple model that could become self-funding."

Early in WorkerBee.TV's development Stevens weathered what could have been a crushing disruption. "We had the option to initially design the business model around trade magazines or associations. I picked trade magazines," Stevens recalls. When the recession hit in 2008, Stevens realized that the magazine industry was going to suffer bitterly.

"While we were trying to convince people to paint the barn a beautiful red, they were screaming that the barn was on fire. My top clients were filing for chapter 11 bankruptcy. They were hit with a perfect storm. The industry consolidated at overinflated prices. The market dropped so all of the money calls were on, and the advertising space for magazines was falling like a rock. Fortunately, I took my dad's advice and didn't hesitate to make a change. We shifted our focus to associations, and we have not looked back. It was a great decision. As the business has grown, Association TV® represents our platform and services for the association marketplace, while WorkerBee.TV is the name and brand for our corporate offerings.

My first association customer, the Material Handling Equipment Distributors Association (MHEDA), is still a wonderful client. This relationship embodies the qualities I enjoy most about being an entrepreneur and working in the association community," says Stevens. "The MHEDA is progressive and member focused. They love to think outside the box. They've challenged us to help them solve some interesting problems.

"For example," continues Stevens, "recruiting top talent is currently challenging for their member companies due to a strong economy and because the average person isn't familiar with the supply chain industry. When you make a purchase on Amazon and the item magically appears on your doorstep the next day, you don't think about the complex voyage your package made through the supply chain. To help job seekers understand the career options, we produced a video that documents every step in the journey of a camera from the customer's first click online to the camera's timely and safe arrival at the destination and all the opportunities for employment along the way. Members can download this video and use it in their employee recruitment and awareness campaigns. These are the kind of collaborative partnerships that make our work both interesting and rewarding."

Evaluate Trends Early

At the core of Stevens's father's advice is the need to predict the writing on the wall before it is written. "I've been in technology my entire life," Stevens says. "When I was younger, I didn't realize how rapidly the industry was cycling. Products and services are launched, explode, and die as quickly as fireworks. But with experience, you become good at spotting the trends. Sometimes we look like we're salmon swimming in the opposite direction from others because we know that having a blind eye to the future is leading the fish that are following the school to a bad end."

Social media is one example of a popular trend that in Stevens's opinion also poses a threat. "Associations have been conditioned to think of social media as integral to their marketing plans," he advises. "We are now hearing about the security breaches and lawsuits and the influence of organizational data on advertising sales. By giving Facebook, YouTube, Twitter, and LinkedIn access to your content, you are inviting them to use your data to learn more about your members than you know. They can also use that information to monetize access and create competitive and personalized models to compete with your association."

Helping clients evaluate trends and stay ahead of the curve is an important part of Stevens's business relationships. "We are always considering how to make it easier, more efficient, and less costly," he says. "Video is great because people get immediate and measurable feedback. I collect the kudos we receive, and at our holiday party I read the comments to our team and their guests. The compliments help the team connect with our clients and recognize everyone's impact. That's why we do what we do. Yes, we get paid for it, but the real benefit comes from supporting our clients."

Get Out of the Way

Passing that enthusiasm on to his employees is one of the perks Stevens gets from being a leader. "Mentoring and watching people grow is inspiring," he says. "I learned a long time ago, a team can do so much more than any individual. We hire for culture first and skills second, knowing that this new employee must gel with the team if we are to continue to grow and be successful.

"If you have team members who understand and believe in the organization's vision and want to leverage their skills against your purpose, then you can truly empower them. I'm always amazed at how quickly employees pick up the ball and run. When I was extremely involved in volunteering for my association, I was on the phone constantly or traveling. Staff members would come to ask me a question, and I could see how disappointed they were that I wasn't available. I told them that if they could stand behind their decision, so could I. After awhile they became comfortable working more independently. We grew 30 percent during that period. I realized that I had become a bottleneck and had to get out of the way. It's completely changed my management style. Now I am more of a cheerleader and a coach, making sure that my staff has the resources and the clarity of our vision to succeed. My team leaders at WorkerBee.TV know I am always available for discussion. But most importantly, they understand that I trust their judgment."

Stevens describes himself as a servant leader. "We're an upside-down pyramid. I work for management. Management works for the front line, and the front line works for the client. In my opinion, that's how it should be," he says. "The company is not a hierarchy.

We don't have a lot of layers. It's a structure that preserves accountability. You have ownership of your decisions. If help is needed, assistance is available. This may sound risky, but if you have a culture of quality, backed by a process of quality, then you don't need to rely on oversight or bureaucracy.

"Customer service is everyone's job," Stevens remarks. "If you need a department to keep customers happy, that's a problem. I recently gave a talk at an Association Media and Publishing conference about how to increase publishing revenue from events. A woman in the audience raised her hand and said, 'I'm the magazine editor. Should this be my job?' I replied, 'I don't know if you will like my answer. In this day and age, why aren't you a multimedia editor? Why would you release a great story in just one format when it can be told on so many venues in different ways? Similarly, why would you have a customer service department?' Our upside-down pyramid creates accountability. It allows us to be responsive and friendly."

Hire Right

Stevens is adamant that work should be fun. "I joke that you only have to work half days here. What you do with the other 12 hours is up to you," he laughs. "The amount of time we spend together makes a shared vision and an effective hiring policy critical. If you let a 'me' person into a 'we' culture you are asking for trouble. We do team interviews, and when we vote to bring on a new employee, every person has responsibility for the new hire's success. It's not easy getting a job here, but when someone joins the team, we don't have to worry about culture and fit.

"I learned that lesson the hard way. When your gut tells you that an employee isn't going to make it, you should address the issue immediately. The first company that I acquired in Vancouver, Canada, had a staffer who was extremely talented but equally toxic," recalls Stevens. "He thought that he was untouchable because he was so skilled. When I finally let him go, people asked me what took so long. Ever since I've been extremely careful."

Putting emotions aside in favor of logic is another skill that Stevens developed with business experience. "We were so successful when we opened our first company in Winnipeg that I thought we should open offices in Calgary and Edmonton, Canada. To make things really exciting, we would launch both sites on the same day. That reasoning, which was completely based on emotion, was a disaster. Because I was so focused on growth, I hired the wrong people. I lost $100,000 in less than 90 days. I also realized how much knowledge was only in our heads and not formalized in a process. I closed both offices. We went back to the drawing board, and three years later we successfully rolled out in seven different locations, before being acquired."

Change at the Rate of Change

Helping his clients view their environment through the sharp lens of objectivity is a priority for Stevens. He believes that growing member retention, recruitment, and revenue in the current climate is challenging, to say the least. A cluster of social and economic issues are altering the association landscape. "Every eight seconds a baby boomer retires," he notes. "The digital generation coming into the workforce is accustomed to getting much of their information for free in bite-sized formats. Social media is using artificial intelligence to build new revenue streams. These changes are happening at an accelerated rate. But the association model is designed to change slowly.

"If you want to go out of business, don't change at the rate of change," Stevens says. "So much of what associations do today is analogue. The big-ticket events are in person. Many groups still print a magazine. In that scenario, all of the best content only hits approximately 15 percent of the audience. Video and other electronic content allow owners to format the information for different tasks and platforms. A 45-minute presentation can be repurposed as both a three-minute micro-learning session and a thirty-second social media promotion. With just one piece of content, you've created a sales funnel from social channels back to the accredited learning program. Soliciting sponsorship could allow you to monetize the same product twice."

Stevens sees the biggest benefit of being digital as the ability to measure results. "You know exactly how many new leads you've turned into members," he says. "You can measure engagement, satisfaction, and revenue. But many associations are still asking sponsors to support activities for which success can't be evaluated. It's impossible to count the sales leads you received from having your logo on a lanyard or a sign on the door. When the 60-year-old chief marketing officer retires, the new 35-year-old executive is going to say, 'I can't buy it if I can't measure it.' Associations that are empowered to change are seeing incredible gains, but organizations stuck sitting on the eggs so they won't break are at risk."

Helping associations thrive online energizes Stevens. "I've been working with the Retail Council of Canada. Retail is one of the industries that is being most severely disrupted by Amazon and other online competitors. The members need their association to educate them more than ever before. We are going to launch a biweekly event called Conference All Year Long."

The CEO of the Retail Council of Canada was instrumental in ensuring that change could occur swiftly. "She invited me to give a presentation to their board. She wanted their input and approval, but she also wanted their involvement to stay at the strategy level so that the staff could move the implementation forward quickly. The directors understood. They empowered the CEO to set three-year goals for the project. We're making sure that the criteria for success is defined and that we can measure our way along this journey. So, without getting into the weeds, the executive board was able to influence execution."

Build a Deep Bench

A strategic board fuels productivity, but sometimes the roadblocks are internal. "I'm amazed at the amount of turnover in associations," Stevens says. "Decisions can be frozen for months during a search. If a year goes by, the organization may fall dangerously behind. I believe successful associations will strive for a better balance between employees and outsourcing. Outsourcing can actually be more predictable. Contract workers know they have to deliver immediate value. Having a deep bench of talent also ensures continuity and seamless service. When a videographer, writer, or editor goes on vacation it doesn't affect our clients because of our global portfolio of freelancers.

"Outside talent can also help to benchmark state-of-the-art performance." Stevens jokes, "I didn't know I was a lousy golfer until I discovered par. Seriously though, you don't always have time to compare yourself to best practices. Freelancers, who are continually sharpening their saws, make associations better."

The goal in hiring and building a team is to create a culture of excellence. "CEOs need to be change agents," says Stevens. "They should be servant leaders who empower the front line. I understand that CEOs must travel and learn, but I worry that their knowledge isn't passed on to the team. There is often a gap between the CEO's vision and the way the front line operates."

Be Your Best Self

"There is still a huge need for associations and continued opportunity for success," says Stevens. "But the demand that you be the best in the world at what you do is increasing daily. Both businesses and associations need to differentiate, hyper-niche and, when appropriate, consolidate. Get critical mass however you can. I believe that my dad's wisdom is not only timeless, it becomes more relevant as change accelerates. The best version of yourself is the one that you are constantly re-creating. If you are unable to say that you are executing that vision better than anyone else, you'll need to find another blue ocean to swim in."

Topics for Group Discussion

Do organizations really need to change as frequently as Stevens says they do?

- Are there drawbacks to frequent change?
- Is your organization equipped to quickly pivot when necessary?

Is the upside-down pyramid the right organizational model for the future?

- On a scale of 1 to 10, how hierarchical is your organization?
- What are the benefits of an upside-down organizational chart?
- What are the drawbacks?

Do you agree with Stevens that social media is a competitor?

- If yes, why? And how is it a threat?
- If no, explain why not.

What is the role of freelance talent in your organization?

- What are the pros and cons of using freelancers?
- What is the appropriate mix of full-time and freelance support?
- What cultural adjustments are needed to integrate freelancers into an organization?

Meet Association TV®/WorkerBee.TV

WorkerBee.TV started in 2007 and is based in Winnipeg, Canada. Their video and multimedia platform and services model allow associations of all sizes to deploy video strategically against key objectives and positively impact retention, recruitment, and revenue. Their passion is to make video simple and effective for all associations and to elevate the relevancy of each association with its current and future membership.

WorkerBee.TV has twenty-five full-time employees and a network of videographers globally who can respond to special filming needs, from a half-day interview to full multi-person conferences and livestreaming. Today, video also makes going multimedia easy, leveraging the growth in podcasts, blogs, and visual social media posts to drive awareness and engagement.

Get to Know Dan

- **My favorite people**—Are in my 28-year-old entrepreneurial forum group that meets monthly. They have helped me be a better entrepreneur, parent, spouse, and person, and I hope I have contributed to their success as a person in some way. Because they certainly have contributed to mine.
- **My most memorable mea**l—Was a beautiful, ocean-side, outdoor restaurant in Acapulco, Mexico, where I proposed

to my wife of more than thirty-four years. The food was so good that she said yes!

- **I've always wanted to**—Travel and learn and have been fortunate to have seen much of this world, but there is still so much left to experience.
- **I'll never forget**—The importance of my father's letter and the increased relevance it has in today's ever-changing world. Anyone or any organization can be disrupted, and we must use today's success to prepare for tomorrow's change or we won't make it to many tomorrows. Change with purpose can be very fun and rewarding, and I hope I can pass forward to my three adult daughters those invaluable lessons from my father and all the people I have learned from and continue to learn along this amazing journey of life.

CHAPTER 18: CHOMKO

AN OPERATING SYSTEM FOR INVENTION

Roy Chomko, CEO, Adage Technologies

"Vision without traction is merely hallucination."—Gino Wickman

How many people know this origin story? In 1970, Bill Gates and two partners launched Traf-O-Data, a moderately successful company that wrote software to create reports for traffic engineers. The rest is, of course, history. Roy Chomko, CEO of Adage Technologies, can tell you about Microsoft's beginnings and a lot more information technology (IT) lore.

When Chomko was in fourth grade his father, who owned a software company, introduced him to a mini-computer and the Digital Equipment Corporation VT100. The idea was for Roy to learn programming. At the time, he was more interested in playing Space Invaders or watching Star Trek. However, that experience was the beginning of a lifelong fascination with technology.

An early compulsion to repair, replace, and tinker also contributed to Chomko's entrepreneurial career path. "We had a big yard and a lawn tractor that always broke down. So, as a kid, I discovered that I like fixing things," Chomko recalls. "I also realized that I enjoy helping people."

Adage Technologies, which provides digital strategy, user interface/user experience (UI/UX) design, web development, and marketing automation, combines all Chomko's interests. "Our technology practice revolves around building products and helping our clients achieve their goals," he says. "We complete a project and release it into the community, and our work gets used every day by a large number of people. That's where I find my passion."

Be Patient

"Ninety-nine percent of business start-ups are not about getting rich fast," Chomko advises. "Even when a company seems to be an overnight success, the ideas behind it may have been percolating for years—which brings to mind that Microsoft story. I admire Gates and the way he built his company and is now using his resources to do good in the world."

Adage is Chomko's third business. The first was a networking and infrastructure company that sold and installed wide and local area networks. Following that initiative, he and three partners launched a web development and e-commerce company that was a precursor to Adage. It was 1999 and signs of recession were already surfacing. Then came the dot.com stock market crash in March 2000, followed by the attack on the World Trade Center in New York City on September 11, 2001. The impact of both events was devastating to the technology industry.

Chomko and his partners had to decide how to position their company in a precarious economic and social environment. The group was divided on strategy, and Chomko and another like-minded partner split off to start Adage. "We didn't feel that the other folks were looking at the reality that 2001 was bringing," Chomko notes. "It was a big adjustment. We took Avaya and Lucent Technologies with us as our two customers. We had a purchase order that was intended to keep us going for half a year. Just one month into the contract, the client called and said, 'Rip up the purchase order and bill us for what we owe.' Their stock had hit bottom, and the employees were all taking early retirement."

Adage stayed afloat but continued to experience growing pains. "We had five employees for five years, and those years were tough. There were times, even during the first ten years, when I thought if I had stayed in technology sales, I could have been making more money and working less," says Chomko. "But I guess that showed me that profit wasn't my highest priority. I believe that you need the persistence and patience to keep on working toward your goal, even when success seems illusive. Making money, for me, is secondary to wanting to innovate and create."

Associations and nonprofits have long been prominent on Adage's client list. "Ten years ago, we built a web application for the American Hospital Association," Chomko says. "That project opened our eyes to the association market. Of course, Chicago, Illinois, is also home to lots of 501(c)(3)s." The fact that the company has chosen to target those human-centered segments of the market fits Chomko's leadership style and his approach to business.

Put People First

While many independent business owners are laser focused on products, Chomko's employees and his customers are his top priority. "I don't think you can survive in a service business if that's not a goal," he advises. "People imagine that if they have a great product it will supersede other obstacles. To some extent, that's true, but at the end of the day if you're not making the customer happy, you're not going to last long."

As a computer geek, Chomko shatters the stereotype of the introverted coder lost in esoteric logic. Relationship building is a skill that comes naturally to him. "I'm a people person," he says. "I find everybody interesting in their own way. I love going to conferences and networking. I'm always open to meeting new people, and I'm inspired by helping my staff and our clients achieve their goals."

Recruiting employees whose values match his own and the company's means Chomko is able to manage more by example than by directive. "Everyone's strength is also their weakness," he says. "I love to collaborate and build consensus, but I'm a pretty hands-off manager. So, I try to find people who share my passions, vision, and goals. I don't really enjoy the supervisory aspects of management, but follow-up and accountability are important." Chomko believes that if employees are a good fit with Adage culture, they will also be successful in a more fluid environment.

The fact that for eight consecutive years Adage has been rated among the best places to work in Illinois is proof that the company is finding the right people. "We have a very involved hiring process," Chomko explains. "It starts with an interview with the recruiting team and moves through conversations with managers, technology testing and, in the case of executive staff, a final more social meeting over coffee or lunch.

"Along that journey, we're checking to make sure that the candidate's skills and attributes align with our core values. Each interview includes a series of questions that we rank according to how closely the answers match our standards. We're looking for people who are passionate about technology and who love to innovate and create. But we're also seeking good ambassadors. That quality involves being able to present yourself professionally to our customers and demonstrating the kind of strong service orientation we advocate—it's a willingness to put the customer first."

Follow Your Own Advice

Over time, Adage has created a culture that makes room for the spontaneity to innovate and build but provides the discipline necessary to execute. This balance has come through trial and error and experience. "We are constantly inventing new products," says Chomko. "We found that during the development process, many of our projects were being passed around from one team to another. Time was being wasted as a result of repetition and replication of effort.

"That problem reached a tipping point when we were working on a seat selection product for performing arts organizations. About twenty large groups, including Lyric Opera of Chicago, the Chicago Symphony Orchestra, and the Metropolitan Opera in New York City were potential customers for this product. Because the work kept getting passed back and forth between teams, our timeline fell behind. We didn't take the advice that we give to our customers—stick to the scope and have clearly defined responsibilities.

"The project took three times longer than the initial estimate. To address that challenge, we created a product development team. That group now handles all the product requests. Now there are better checks and balances to ensure that we're not wasting time. A centralized approach gives everyone greater control. We're taking our own advice and documenting the scope, focusing on one team and using a scrum model, a project management tool for software development. We've also become more diligent about having periodic meetings to assess progress."

Get an Operating System

"Another tool that's made us more effective is the Entrepreneurial Operating System (EOS) that was developed by Gino Wickman," says Chomko. "Wickman's book, *Traction: Get a Grip on Your Business*, and his other writings outline a simple process that entrepreneurs can follow to ensure that any organization is being run effectively. Companies with between 5 and 250 employees are the target market for this system.

"This is an option that other organizations seeking to adopt a more innovative approach might consider," Chomko advises. "I've often thought that the model could work effectively in an association environment. Executive directors seem to change fairly frequently, even in the most stable organizations. The EOS is a proven template that is easy to use, and I think that's what many leaders need, especially someone who doesn't have deep experience in running an organization."

Chomko credits the EOS with helping Adage stick to simple habits for good business. "For example," he says, "our meetings of the leadership team weren't systematic enough and didn't occur on a regular schedule. We didn't discuss the good news first or have score cards. Although we were following some of the steps, we hadn't orchestrated our processes comprehensively. Our operations were too casual. That's one thing I've learned. You need a model. For us, the EOS is a blueprint that provides the structure to move forward.

"This system has helped us pinpoint what we want to do and where we want to go and communicate those goals to the team. There are a number of similar programs available, and from an entrepreneur's standpoint, these tools are worth the investment. When your company runs like a business you don't have silos, and you provide a structure around which people can organize."

Match Mission to Members

Silos, Chomko notes, sometimes prevent associations from fulfilling their missions and serving their members' best interests. The messaging may be communicated differently across the organization and may have become less relevant. "Every department believes that it is delivering on the mission," says Chomko, "but no one is focused on how those goals relate to the end user. From the technological perspective, this can translate to a small organization with three different customer relations management systems or a fractured web environment with ten different sites for a $15 million organization. Each team is acting on a vision that projects that group's vantage point."

The board can create yet another silo that needs to be better integrated into the organizational model. "Oftentimes board members are industry leaders who don't have experience running a business. Medical specialties are a good example. Most doctors probably don't lead their own organizations. Managing a nonprofit is a very different animal. I remember sitting in a board meeting in which one of the directors insisted that it was essential to maintain an outdated listserv. That type of specialized requirement from an individual member can drive the leadership to make decisions that aren't always the best for the organization."

Switching that paradigm, that is, bringing members into the spotlight but out of operational decisions, is a more effective approach for the future. "We're already seeing a much heavier focus on member needs and concerns, and IT is central to helping associations deliver better value to their constituents," notes Chomko. "Digital strategies are tailor-made to serve a distributed user group that comes together once or twice a year. I think that conferences are still really important. I enjoy every conference that I attend. But online solutions will be helping people stay connected.

Future successful associations are going to be member-centered and digitally driven."

Employee satisfaction will also be a critical consideration for associations that want to thrive over the next decade. "If we don't make our employees happy, we won't have happy customers," says Chomko. "I think of Adage as a concentric circle. The innermost circle is our values, then come our employees, and then our customers."

It's the CEO's job to nurture those important staff and member relationships and to understand the technology that can take them to the next level. "Beyond that," says Chomko, "it's hard to predict what kind of leader will be most successful. I do believe that it's important to have taken risks and tried and failed. This is my third business. The other two were only moderately successful. But listening to the lessons of failure and making every misstep bring me closer to my goals was an invaluable experience. That's how patience and persistence hones leaders and prepares them for success."

Topics for Group Discussion

Does your organization have a structure that creates traction?

- Where are you weak?
- Where are you strong?
- Do you need help?

Are members taking a back seat to mission in your organization?

- How is your mission serving the membership?
- Are you offering lip service or authenticity?
- What is the evidence that your mission is being effectively executed?

What is the predominate management style in your organization: more hands-off or more hands-on?

- Is that working for you?
- If yes, why?
- If no, why not?

What is the balance between innovation and process in your organization?

- Are you creating space for innovation?
- Are you offering structure for execution?

Meet Adage

Founded in 2001, Adage Technologies is an e-commerce web design and development firm in downtown Chicago, Illinois. Adage has consistently been recognized as one of Chicago's 101 Best and Brightest Companies to Work For, one of the Best Places to Work in Illinois, and on the *Inc. Magazine* 5000 list of the fastest-growing privately held companies in the United States. Adage is a team of strategic, creative, and technical professionals who partner with their clients to solve business problems and meet meaningful goals. It's their team-oriented approach that truly drives them to win awards, work with prestigious clients, and break ground with exciting new technology.

Get to Know Roy

- **My favorite people**—Bill Gates, Mark Cuban, Elon Musk, my mom.
- **My most memorable meal**—Diners, drive-ins, and dives. An Ecuadoran restaurant in Des Moines, Iowa. We did not expect much and thoroughly enjoyed it!
- **I've always wanted to**—Ski in the Alps and South America.

- **I'll never forget**—Being buzzed by two F-15 fighter jets while hiking at 14,000 feet.

CHAPTER 19: GIBSON

SELLING THE MISSION

Brent Gibson, MD, MPH, FACPM, CCHP-P; Chief Health Officer, National Commission on Correctional Health Care, and Managing Director, NCCHC Resources, Inc.

> *"I don't look to jump over 7-foot bars. I look around for 1-foot bars that I can step over."—Warren Buffett*

When Brent Gibson started investing, he also learned some valuable life lessons. "I was terrified early on because I didn't know anything about the markets. But I realized that most neophytes don't. Now, I'm confident enough to be an active trader. Taking over my portfolio taught me about decision-making, business, and entrepreneurship," he notes. As an investor, Gibson is comfortable with calculated risk. "You realize that you won't get every bet right. Sometimes you are going to lose. But that shouldn't stop you from trying," he advises. "Abandoning your strategy is a much more dangerous approach."

Gibson is a licensed physician who trained and is board certified in occupational medicine. He began his career in the U.S. Army. A personal risk was the catalyst that put him on the path to his current job with the National Commission on Correctional Health Care (NCCHC). "As soon as my military obligation was over, I took a position in the private sector," he recalls. "When you work in government, you become accustomed to predictable procedures and outcomes. I assumed that, just like the military, people would watch out for me and help me along. If things didn't work, I imagined there would be another job coming down the pike. I quickly learned that in business, there is no parachute. That job wasn't what I hoped it would be. But when I look back, it was a gamble I had to take in order to grow. My tactics may have failed, but the strategy was a success. I had to press through and go out on my own. One thing led to another, and here I am twelve years later."

In his current position, Gibson wears two hats. "I serve as the chief health officer at NCCHC, which is the umbrella organization of four distinct 501(c)(3)s. NCCHC Resources, where I am managing director, is the consulting division. We provide technical assistance to jails and prisons around the country that are facing challenges related to health care.

"At this stage in our corporate development, much of my time is still spent overseeing that technical assistance. For example, if a county transitions from using a health services vendor to learning to operate its own program, we provide expertise to clients in every aspect of the process. Whether it's clinical expertise, human resources, finance, or purchasing, we support our customers as they take on complex initiatives. When a new vendor needs to learn the ins and outs of providing health care in a correctional environment, we assemble an expert team to educate them. Jails and prisons operate very differently from traditional medical settings. We teach our customers how to handle everything from acute care to chronic disease and coordinating with community health providers."

Turn Opportunities Into Revenue

NCCHC Resources is a nimble, innovative partner for its more traditional parent organization. While NCCHC focuses on activities such as accreditation and certification, its Resources affiliate actively seeks new business and identifies gaps where additional services are needed. "We find niches where we can develop programs, and we turn those opportunities into revenue. Ideally, we're developing long-term customers that will provide an ongoing source of support. Those more concrete revenue streams are very good for the business," says Gibson. As the enterprise grows, Gibson also develops the new systems that are needed to manage a larger, more complex workload. "We're supervising multiple contractors across projects and many different statements of work. We are constantly called on to solve unique problems. For me, being entrepreneurial is centered on finding new ways to support our mission to ensure high-quality health care."

Most physicians, Gibson points out, think of being entrepreneurial as finding strategies to grow a traditional clinical practice. "In our case," he says, "innovation is tied to identifying how we keep our mission sustainable. That's what I like about the nonprofit world; our revenue goes back into programs, and in some cases, supports components of the larger business that may not be margin positive in any given year."

Throughout Gibson's career, he has found inspiration and motivation in his faith and his large, close-knit family. "Whatever your faith, if you're not aiming high and working for someone besides yourself, you'll be lost sooner or later. That's the North Star. Down to earth and practically speaking, my wife and I have been married for twenty-two years, and we have six children. Our youngest has significant intellectual and physical disabilities. Taking care of the family creates a fire in me to excel professionally. While everyone needs to pay the bills and put food on the table, I have a higher level of intensity than many. That passion contributes to a laser focus on my work as a public health physician and entrepreneur."

Mentors in the nonprofit sector have been another source of support. "Jim Pavletich, NCCHC's former CEO, has had a fantastic set of experiences working in health care organizations," Gibson says. "Jim wants his colleagues to succeed and his staff to shine. His example has helped me as I manage my own team.

"Over time, I've learned how to trust and delegate. Whereas my military background was focused on command and control at the junior level, as I've grown, I've come to understand that with the right people on board you can manage more broadly. The ability to take a half a step back and see the big picture is something that I cultivate. But you've got to be able to adjust your style with each changing work environment. Every company has a distinct set of demands. The flexibility to adapt to the situation is important."

Gibson's position calls for an entrepreneurial approach in a culture that presents some challenges to that goal. The organization is an unlikely incubator for innovation. Gibson observes, "Medicine and corrections are both risk-averse." Frequent communication with NCCHC's various audiences helps Gibson successfully navigate this cautious environment. "Of all the stakeholders, often the most reluctant to accept a change are internal," he advises. When he needs to convince a colleague or board member about the importance of launching a new initiative, Gibson must demonstrate how opportunity can mitigate risk and explain the drawbacks of allowing too much prudence to stifle initiative.

Be a Competitor

The NCCHC is not a typical association. There are no members. As Gibson describes the organization, "We are a very serious accrediting business. Writing and surveying for standards compliance is a primary activity. With this kind of structure, there are limited sources of revenue. We need to create new strategies to generate financial resources. Being sustainable is as essential for a nonprofit as it is for any other business.

"All of my major competitors, with a few exceptions, are for-profit companies. We've got to get out there and do a better job in an entrepreneurial way," Gibson says. Nonprofits cannot continue to believe that their space is off limits to competition. Corporations, such as major airlines and banks, already successfully model the membership concept. Gibson does see one significant edge that NCCHC has over for-profits. "Think about the Newman's Own brand and similar products. Running a business as a charitable endeavor is an effective selling point. People are happier to part with their money when they know it's being invested in a cause that is noble and good. At NCCHC Resources, we sell our technical services wrapped around the core of our long-standing mission. Our competition is in business to make money as a primary objective (and there is nothing wrong with that). But we serve our mission by operating profitably."

NCCHC Resources fits the model of a start-up within a larger association. "We run a lean operation," Gibson notes. "This structure meets our needs because we don't want too much bureaucratic friction. We like to keep the board small and nimble so that we can stay focused on finding and developing customers. Our meetings are minimal, but the reporting is very transparent. We don't have any committees because we don't need them." Gibson believes that more associations could benefit from this approach. "The mission typically overshadows profitability. But you need to embed people who will be creative and take risks so that good things happen. For example, the U.S. Army is a huge system with little pockets of high-level innovation where ideas and inventions can be developed."

Deliberately identifying new or additional customer services is one path that associations and other nonprofits can take toward growth. Gibson says, "Historically at NCCHC, all technical assistance was based on support for accreditation, and we didn't focus on margin. It became evident that, due to the complexity of the operating environment, there were services outside our realm of expertise that were not being provided. We were perfectly positioned to contract with experts who could solve these complex problems for our customers. You have a choice to either say, 'We can't help you,' or you can figure out how to fill in the missing pieces. It may take some mental wrangling. But the bottom line is, don't be afraid of a calculated risk."

Acknowledge a New Environment

Gibson sees associations moving away from traditional models. "Like membership dues, certification and accreditation programs may not remain the reliable revenue generators that they always have been. I read about challenges to these programs almost daily, and their value is under scrutiny by some. I feel as though growing those services may take longer than business realities demand and so it is a good idea to always look for other sources of revenue. More generally, much of what associations have typically done—the convening of people and ideas for mutual interest—is now provided for free on social media. Personally, I'm a member of the professional society for my specialty, which I do enjoy. I worked for many years to earn a credential from that association. Now my primary interest in membership is to maintain the credential, and I'm not sure about that document's value in my current marketplace. What then is the value of membership? If I struggle with this, others certainly do too.

"Associations need people who are cutting-edge and aggressive in order to remain viable and compete," advises Gibson. "We've made great strides in improvements in compensation, and nonprofit benefits have always been good. But if you look at the salaries of the big nonprofit CEOs, they are still a tiny fraction of what is paid to for-profit executives. If associations want to attract the best talent, they must operate more like the corporate sector without compromising their nonprofit values."

Recruiting and retaining top performers is rapidly becoming an entirely new ballgame. "The sense of loyalty that used to exist is disappearing," says Gibson. "One of the biggest motivations for me to join the military was the idea of belonging to an organization that serves others and makes me a better person. People aren't seeking that type of fulfillment from one company anymore. They stay with an employer for a couple of years and then move on." Gibson sees more employees looking beyond their professional lives for social and emotional gratification.

With competition for both ideas and expertise growing throughout the nonprofit sector, CEOs need to embrace the qualities required for success in a more Darwinian marketplace. Unassailable business acumen and the ability to develop knowledge-based organizations in which strategy is driven by data and informed intuition will be fundamental. "In most cases, a business decision is not a math problem with a single solution," says Gibson. "CEOs will need to be able to take timely, decisive action to move their organizations forward. Above all," he notes, "it will be the leaders who are charged with elevating their organization's stature within the business community. There's a tendency to diminish the value of nonprofit work. It's up to those executives to ensure that the focus on mission over revenue increases the respect for their institutions and the job they do promoting the public good."

The lines between the association and the corporate world are blurring. Gibson believes associations can find new relevance in creating innovative ways to fill those gaps. "Future viability lies in looking more broadly at where businesses are either not present or not functioning well and occupying those spaces. We need the courage to experiment with innovative ideas, new relationships, and unexpected partnerships," Gibson says. He'd like to see associations stop checking the rearview mirror. He believes they can move beyond their current purpose of professional collaboration and advancement to a more proactive vision. "It's good to understand where you came from," Gibson says. "But you really need to focus on where you are going."

Topics for Group Discussion

What are some of the differences between how for-profits and nonprofits operate?

- Are there ways in which your organization operates like a for-profit?
- If so, would it be beneficial to expand those areas?
- How can associations operate more like businesses without compromising their values?

Are there gaps in service that your organization could fill?

- Do you have a process for identifying those new sources of revenue?

Do you use your mission as a sales tool?

- Is your mission carried through your branding initiatives?

Meet NCCHC and NCCHC Resources

The NCCHC establishes standards for health services in correctional facilities, operates a voluntary accreditation program for institutions that meet those standards, produces and disseminates resource publications, conducts educational conferences, and offers a certification program for correctional health professionals.

A nonprofit organization, NCCHC Resources, Inc., is a boutique not-for-profit management consulting firm that works to strengthen NCCHC's mission: to improve the quality of health care in prisons, jails, and juvenile detention and confinement facilities.

Get to Know Brent

- **My favorite people**—Include St. John Paul the Great—a passionate and erudite man who helped heal the rifts of post-communist Europe, focused on youth, and set the standard for modern spiritual leaders. My wife Julia, an exceptional woman who trekked across the globe to marry me, she typifies calculated risk-taking and selfless sacrifice. I learn from her every day.
- **My most memorable meal**—Was at Pink Chilli in Goa, India. Two meals, actually. This little bistro served fresh everything with an emphasis on fresh seafood and local treats, including a variety of good Indian beers. Chock full of deliberately stereotypical Indian kitsch, it was an absolutely fantastic experience.
- **I've always wanted to**—Sit on a warm, non-crowded beach somewhere and do nothing for days. . .still waiting.

- **I'll never forget**—My first visit to Rome back in 2016. I could not believe the high density of places of worship, relics, and Renaissance art and architecture, and the near-literal chunks of history strewn about everywhere. It's truly remarkable.

CHAPTER 20: CARDEN AND MARTIN

CREATING THEIR OWN SUCCESS

Teri Carden and Ben Martin, CAE

Co-Founders, 100Reviews

> *"The only way to do great work is to love what you do. If you haven't found it yet, keep looking. Don't settle."—Steve Jobs*

Teri Carden and Ben Martin are partners in business, in life, and most significantly, in spirit. Their latest venture, 100Reviews, is the product of their mutual fascination with technology and their commitment to advancing the association community.

Carden, who describes herself as a "girl geek in normal girl's clothing," grew up in a family that prized creativity and innovation. "My dad was an entrepreneur," she says. "He was a postal worker, but he also built the home we grew up in and ran his own outdoor family games business. The early experience of watching him begin a project and see it through to the final product planted the desire in me to follow his example." Carden identifies that need to build and create as a primary driver in her professional life. "My dad's 70 years old now," she says, "and he still runs his own T-shirt company out of his back patio in Florida."

Adding to Carden's perspective, Martin notes that the ability to see things that others don't and the willingness to risk failure to realize a vision are characteristics the two share. He points to Thomas Edison's comment, "I have not failed. I've just found 10,000 ways that won't work," as an apt description of their entrepreneurial mind-set.

Begin with the Goal in Mind

"I believe you have to start with the end in mind," says Carden. "You need to decide what you want to accomplish. We asked ourselves if we were going to shoot for a Fortune 500 company, or if we wanted to create something more attainable." Carden and Martin opted for what they call a lifestyle business. The scale of their company allows them to pursue their passion for advancing associations and still have time to enjoy their family and travel to the many places on their adventure bucket list.

The couple were both fortunate to first experience the rush that comes from innovation without the risk that new business owners typically face. "I had a job with the Virginia Association of REALTORS that presented many opportunities to experiment with new projects and initiatives in a safe environment," Martin recalls. "When you're getting a paycheck, what's the worst that can happen? You might get fired. But there are other jobs. I was pushed out of the nest when the software company that I was working for was acquired. Then, I was able to take what I had learned in a protected space and apply it to my own business."

Chocolate chips and cookie dough played a starring role in teaching Carden about running a company. "I got my initial chance at being creative, managing my own products, and watching revenue grow as the general manager for the Christie Cookie in Nashville, Tennessee" says Carden. "There were eleven locations plus the corporate office, and I was the second in command. My boss had been building the business for twenty-five years, and he wanted to lighten his responsibilities. After I traveled to Italy to learn how to make gelato, he asked me to manage the branding. As a young professional, bringing a product to life like that was really exciting," says Carden.

The cookie business wasn't all sugar and spice though. "Working for a cookie company during the Christmas season was insane. I was sleeping under my desk and living on NoDoz and oatmeal raisin cookies." The fatigue is apparent in Carden's voice as she remembers the experience. "When the team arrived at 5 a.m., I was still wearing the same clothes I had been wearing when they left the night before

I decided to take a much-needed break to spend time with my children. After just a few weeks all the laundry was done, the drawers were organized, the house was pristine, and I was bored. So, I got a job with the Florida Society of Association Executives."

The association industry was a good fit for Carden for many years to follow, but she couldn't ignore the constant tug to create something of her own. She found a happy medium when the Association for Retail Environments allowed her to work on contract. "I was able to balance building a new business with having the safety net of an association job. It was a lot of luck," she says.

Build the Product that Makes You Proud

Carden's first product, ReviewMyAMS, grew out of her curiosity about technology and her experience managing the purchase and installation of a variety of electronic platforms. She had firsthand knowledge about the high stakes involved in selecting an association management system (AMS) and wanted to help other leaders make this critical decision.

Like a true entrepreneur, Carden also saw what others didn't. Yelp, TripAdvisor, Amazon, and a plethora of other review sites were available to consumers. But business-to-business (B2B) clients didn't have many options for assessing purchases as significant as an AMS. She set out to fill that need. With input from Martin and other industry colleagues, she created an online site where users could critique their AMS systems and potential buyers could learn from the experiences of others.

The idea caught fire. Association executives were quick to see the value in giving members an opportunity to vet industry products in a structured format. Shortly, Carden was fielding requests to rebrand and repurpose ReviewMyAMS. The offers were tempting. Carden and Martin were eager to grow their business. But they also understood that at this stage of development, the product's value was in the content, not the architecture. The software Carden had created wasn't sophisticated enough to serve multiple customers with a variety of needs.

The couple had to decide whether they were ready to invest the time, effort, and money in building the product the market wanted. "Teri knew that she couldn't hit customer expectations with her current solution," said Martin. "At that point, we decided to create something that we could be proud of."

"We didn't want to build a product that could barely hold up in the marketplace; we wanted to make something that would be loved and that users would be proud of," agrees Carden. "Creating a new service comes with the cost of educating consumers," she notes. "I felt that we were at a safe place with ReviewMyAMS. The time was perfect for us to launch another iteration. 100Reviews is that product. Any association can use the software to install their own review platform proprietary to their industry. We'll know whether we got it right in the first six months of 2019. But so far, so good."

The couple has gone on to develop many other review sites for the association industry, such as ReviewMySpeaker.com, ReviewMyLMS.com, and ReviewMyCommunity.net.

By giving a forum to consumers, who were limited in their ability to interact with each other, and creating an entirely new channel for information and end-user sharing, Carden and Martin also inserted a disruption into the B2B market. They are excited to see how these expanded avenues for communication, data, and revenue will impact buyers and sellers.

"Fail Fast and Fail Small"

No business owner sets out to fail. But most entrepreneurs accept disappointments as part of the game. Whoever coined the phrase "fail fast and fail small" was describing what might be a fledgling venture's best-case scenario. Associations have yet to embrace that mind-set. Martin observes, "Industries are changing so quickly. There is no guarantee of success. You can invest several years in strategizing, and by the time you're ready for implementation, the goalpost will have moved. The luxury of hitting the bull's-eye every time no longer exists. It may be better to take smaller risks and try for a one-in-ten success ratio."

Carden adds, "The associations that do the best pivoting have changed the way they think. They give the staff more control and the power and luxury to take risks. For example, a department could initiate a project using a start-up mentality. The group might have $25,000 to explore developing a new product or service. If they hit on a great concept, they can share the love with the other departments and turn it into something much bigger. It's as if you were designating smaller areas of the association as incubators to build something bigger and better for the whole.

"When somebody creates, whether it's as part of a team or by themselves, it instills pride and ownership. You generate energy that adds a layer of sophistication to the entire project. Giving people the authority to move quickly in a smaller environment leads to success. I have a personal advisory board that I consult for large decisions or ethical issues. They come from all walks of life—some are family, others are teachers, entrepreneurs, investors, and people from my church. But when I'm about to launch a new venture, the decisions are all my own. There's a lot of personal investment. I think the key for associations will be to give people ownership so that they can claim their success and use failure as a learning experience."

Match Risk with Resources

Creating pockets of innovation within an organization should be matched with providing adequate financial resources for experimentation. "Associations can consider allocating a portion of their budgets, say 1 percent, to finding new ideas," says Martin. "Most associations have finite staff resources. You have to balance what you ask employees to do against their core responsibilities." Martin notes that there are multiple ways to slice the innovation pie. "You can allocate a percentage of entrepreneurial time to everyone's job or hire a few people who are devoted to emerging initiatives. It's important to recognize that being a risk-taker is not for everyone. The CEO doesn't need to be an entrepreneur. But they must empower some people in the organization to do that work."

"Association jobs are demanding," says Carden. "Just giving employees mental white space can spark invention. Providing the opportunity for staff to learn more about member perspectives and concerns can also be a source of inspiration. We've seen several associations exporting data from their online communities and analyzing it with artificial intelligence tools to extract member sentiments and find fresh solutions to problems. Instead of playing a guessing game, they're allowing the members to drive the conversation. Doing more listening can also generate ideas for products and services.

"Sunsetting outdated activities and programs frees up resources for research and development," advises Carden. "It's important to have a target end date, which can always change if a project continues to be successful. The challenge is knowing when it's time to end or upgrade. I could not have let ReviewMyAMS stagnate. If I had not made the improvements, someone else would have seized the opportunity to build it with better features, search options, and functionality."

Carden and Martin agree that associations benefit from their unique place in the market. "Associations have the resources to lobby at the state, national, and local level. They are really the only organizations that are equipped to do that," says Martin. "In the future, I think they'll take a broader approach. There will be a shift away from membership towards a more community-oriented perspective. .orgCommunity is a perfect example of that—in that the members come from a number of different sectors."

"Associations are vulnerable to competition on the educational, technological, and engagement fronts," says Carden. "But I also believe they are hungry to try something new. There are tech companies and other ancillary businesses that are committed to supporting this community, and together we'll be around for a long time. But will associations look the same three years from now? I don't think so."

Be Authentic

"I see a lot of yoga pants in the future," laughs Carden. She points to the increasing popularity of virtual meetings and remote work. She believes the changing workforce will have a major impact on the way associations operate. "Millennials will comprise 50 percent of the workforce as of 2020. They will bring greater diversity, and hopefully, we will also see more international workers. Millennials value authenticity. They grew up sharing their lives on social media. Association leaders should embrace this new generation's mind-set and encourage their uniqueness. Authenticity is attractive in leaders. By adopting a more open orientation, CEOs can set themselves, and their organizations, apart from the rest of the business world.

"I have a little wooden plaque that hangs in my kitchen where I can see it all the time. The message embossed on it is this quote from Bob Marley, 'If you love the life you live, you will live a life of love.' When I'm in the rush of business or travel, I stop and think about those words, and I ask myself if that is what I'm doing. The answer for the last five years that I've been my own boss has been a resounding 'Yes.' If you are inspired and motivated, surrounded by people who are smarter than you are, and are eager to keep learning or trying different things, that will empower you to change the world."

Topics for Group Discussion

Who are the innovators and risk-takers on your staff?

- Do you provide the freedom for them to be creative?
- What departments could serve as incubators for new ideas?

- What does giving people the white space to be creative mean?

What does authenticity mean to you?

- Is this a quality that is promoted in your organization?

Could the concept of failing fast and failing small be helpful to your organization?

- How could this idea be implemented with your programs and services?

Does your association have a strategy for attracting and retaining a new generation of employees?

- How have younger employees changed the way your organization operates?

Meet 100Reviews

In the consumer market, customers make buying decisions for restaurants, vacations, and products based on reviews. But most B2B markets lack dedicated review sites where customers have a voice and can read reviews on the products used at work. Meet 100Reviews. The company, located in Nashville, Tennessee, has been in business since October 2016. They are a digital team of two plus Martin and Carden and their development firm.

Get to Know Teri

- **My favorite people**—Ben, of course. My family, especially the strong women. My children, although they are teens so some days they aren't my favorite. Fogdirockstars—you know who you are.

- **My favorite moments in life**—Are when I prank or surprise someone. I have so many great prank stories that make me laugh out loud when I think of them. Just ask me and I'll tell you a few. I also LOVE time at the water. It's good for reflection, creativity, and my soul.
- **I've always wanted to**—Scuba dive, visit Hawaii or... number one—I'd go back in time and become a programmer.
- **I'll never forget**—How lucky I am to have such a wonderful family, community, and network. Truly, I feel like the luckiest girl in the world, and if everyone had the life that I get to have, the world would be a much happier place.

Get to Know Ben

- **My favorite people**—Teri and my kids; the most important people in my world. Every day I feel like I'm becoming more like my mom. My dad died in 1999; I wish I could have him back in my life.
- **My most memorable meal**—Teri and I have traveled to Aruba for New Year's five years in a row. We always order the triple tail fish from Yemanja, a female-owned, woodfire grill. We're committed to learning to create our own version of Nashville Hot Chicken. Wish us luck!
- **I've always wanted to**—Nope. I feel like I've already unlocked every level in the game of life.
- **I'll never forget**—2012.

CONCLUSION

Become a Transformer

We hope that reading these interviews has been as significant a learning experience for you as participating in them was for us. Although each contributor has a unique story, we were struck by the commonality and clarity of their advice to the association community.

Put Technology in Context

Like it or not, technology and business are fraternal twins—different physically but sharing half of each other's DNA. All disruption, innovation, and growth are connected to the digital world, and technology is also rapidly merging with biology. It goes without saying that a digital transformation—or fully integrated software systems—are a critical component of running a successful association. Your software is only as good as its ability to work across platforms and to provide a 360-degree view of your organization's world. Learning how to use the data to develop an intimate understanding of constituents and making business decisions based on that information is the ultimate goal.

However, those systems, along with the connectivity and statistics that they generate, have limited meaning and little impact outside of context. The values that drive how digital solutions are initiated and applied are the true agents of innovation. The transformers we interviewed were unanimous in their opinion that associations will need to make significant behavioral and attitudinal changes in order to keep pace with the speed of business. Taken as a whole, the following qualities represent the context that we believe will be important for associations, or any organization, to adopt in order to make a successful transformation to Association 4.0.

Welcome Risk and Change

Every contributor to this book has an intimate relationship with risk. It's a frenemy they've learned how to manage. Sometimes that involves mitigating the downside, whereas other times it means taking a calculated leap of faith. Either way, there was universal agreement among the contributors that growth and innovation are inextricably tied to risk. To thrive throughout the digital revolution, leaders must find ways to cross minefields as though doing so is a walk in the park. In other words, they must treat risk as a necessary partner with relevance.

Sandy Marsico described the ongoing challenge of balancing risk with growth this way:

> *You need the courage to take chances and the stomach to handle anxiety. With a growing business, things change, but they don't get easier. You have to believe in yourself. You're the one who drives success and encourages others to follow. You're the leader, and you're also the only one who can't give up.*
>
> *I have a budget line for risk. These are not contingency dollars. These funds are designated for experimentation. I don't always know how I'm going to spend the money, but when there is an opportunity, we are ready to seize it. I have another financial strategy that also helps us innovate. When I plan for a new executive level hire, I use profits from the year prior to mentally prepay that salary. That way, the first year is less stressful. It gives a new executive space to get up to speed.*

Allocating financial resources to experimental initiatives is a common practice among this group of entrepreneurs. Most have budget lines that are dedicated to development. Unfortunately, association CEOs seldom have the luxury to make these decisions independently. They must address the added challenge of convincing a board to become more adventurous. Sig VanDamme offered this advice:

> *Preparing a board to tolerate risk is a sales process. To convince you to buy from me, you must believe that I can increase revenue, decrease costs, reduce cycle time, enhance the member experience, and finally, mitigate risk." Leaders must be able to communicate each of those points to both staff and volunteers and be able to present risk within a cognitive framework.*

Boards that are professionally, demographically, and ideologically diverse are more likely to be open to risk tolerance. Joanna Pineda recommends looking outside members' professional expertise to provide a spectrum of opinion and ideas among leaders:

> *I had an interesting conversation with a client about association boards. He was considering the benefits of expanding representation to include expertise from outside the profession. Specifically, he suggested giving experienced association executives a seat at the table.*
>
> *If you don't have leaders with a range of professional backgrounds, there will not be a lot of new thinking. The average pharmacist, librarian, or dentist has limited experience with the challenges that are involved in running an association. It's a good idea to include people from outside your organization's playing field who can introduce a different point of view and push the group forward.*

Ben Martin, CAE observed that not everyone in an organization can, or needs to be, a risk-taker:

> *It's important to recognize that being a risk-taker is not for everyone. The CEO doesn't need to be an entrepreneur. But they must empower some people in the organization to do that work.*

Cultivate Innovation and Problem-Solving

A passion for innovation and problem-solving was universal among our contributors. For them, building solutions is not an occasional activity. It is a way of life that, in some cases, began as early as childhood. We were surprised by the number of people who told us that their parents had also been business owners.

Whether they inherit a gene for invention or not, once they are thrown into the business shark tank, entrepreneurs learn to swim pretty quickly. They also discover that survival means staying ahead of the competition's jaws. Transformers need to imagine the next problem before it surfaces and be willing to test, experiment, and iterate until they find the solution. The concept of a minimum viable product was mentioned frequently in the interviews.

Smart innovators begin with a prototype, a product with just enough features to be attractive, thereby allowing customer response to guide the final design. This often means recalibrating to meet evolving conditions. You don't jump to commitment; you wait for feedback to put a ring on it. Tracy King, MA, CAE, always has her ear tuned to the market. She has learned to accept and grow from the verdict it hands down:

> *Allowing for learning through failure creates the freedom to solve problems instead of checking tasks off a list. We must ruthlessly sift the challenges from the temporary distractions and seek the nuggets of truth in every successful disappointment. Incremental innovation is smart. So is listening deeply to the market and using [minimum viable products] to recalibrate. These are strategies that allow associations to see a real-time picture of their members' needs.*

Association executive Brent Gibson, described how he has been able to be an innovator within a bureaucratic organization:

> *Deliberately identifying new or additional customer services is one path that associations and other nonprofits can take toward growth. Historically at [the National Commission on Correctional Health Care], all technical assistance was based on support for accreditation, and we didn't focus on margin. It became evident that, due to the complexity of the operating environment, there were services outside our realm of expertise that were not being provided. We were perfectly positioned to contract with experts who could solve these complex problems for our customers. You have a choice to either say, 'We can't help you,' or you can figure out how to fill in the missing pieces. It may take some mental wrangling. But the bottom line is, don't be afraid of a calculated risk.*

As a manager of associations, Kim Robinson, CAE believes that by taking an entrepreneurial approach to challenges, organizations can better navigate disruption and change:

> *I believe that the entrepreneurs, who are driven to find solutions and solve problems, are going to provide strategies for success in this new environment. It's an Amazon world. Our members are Amazon customers, and that experience becomes the baseline.*

Be Agile

Reaction, revision, and reinvention are standard operating procedure for entrepreneurs. But all contributors acknowledged the difficulty of operating with that agility inside organizations at which decisions are made by consensus, volunteer leadership changes frequently, and strategy can be subject to a new board chair or president's predilections. Many contributors pointed to the CEO as the person with the power to create an environment that is prepared for and welcomes change. Joey Knecht recommends that leaders turn the focus away from politics and toward business:

> *In addition to inspiration and the drive to succeed, a great CEO has to be a salesperson at heart. They need to approach operations from a product orientation. Leaders must understand how to leverage technology and minimize politics in their organizations. I think a lot of people are tired of the politics that pervades many associations. They see that 2 percent of the membership are driving the bus and the other 98 percent are along for the ride. Executives need to find ways to make participation more equitable and enjoyable.*

Courage was identified by Meg Ward as the essential quality to enable leaders to govern more effectively:

> *CEOs need to be courageous in order to cut through the noise and execute, whether it's implementing a new program or evolving staff skill sets.*

Dan Stevens observes that being a reactive leader is untenable in the digital era:

> *CEOs need to be change agents. They should be servant leaders who empower the front line. I understand that CEOs must travel and learn, but I worry that their knowledge isn't passed on to the team. There is often a gap between the CEO's vision and the way the front line operates.*

Study Business and the Marketplace

There was general agreement that association CEOs should approach leadership from a business perspective and be knowledgeable about events and practices in the corporate world. Reading and networking widely were common habits of our contributors. Many business authors are mentioned throughout the text and several of them, such as Jim Collins, are cited multiple times. Networking groups such as Vistage, Entrepreneurs' Organization, and our own .orgCommunity are resources for inspiration, advice, and studying market trends. Roy Chomko credits a book with helping his business to run more smoothly:

> *Another tool that's made us more effective is the Entrepreneurial Operating System that was developed by Gino Wickman. Wickman's book, Traction: Get a Grip on Your Business, and his other writings outline a simple process that entrepreneurs can follow to ensure that any organization is being run effectively. Companies with between 5 and 250 employees are the target market for this system.*
>
> *This is an option that other organizations seeking to adopt a more innovative approach might consider. I've often thought that the model could work effectively in an association environment.*

A commitment to observing the market and responding quickly to its cues is fundamental to Don Dea's and Hugh Lees's approach to strategy. Lee noted the following:

> *When we started the company, we had over $1 million worth of business doing slides. Forty years ago that was worth something, but I was reading about how these things called personal computers and laptops were going to change the industry.*
>
> *I sat down with the staff and told them we had to be out of the slide business within the next 18 months. I said, 'We're going to replace that million dollars with a thing called PowerPoint.' We changed our entire model. You take a lot of risks, and you're never really positive that you're right. But you have to believe in yourself.*

Co-creation is a strategy for listening to the market by tapping the expertise of a community. Although collective input may be more limited in scope than some approaches, it is rich in feedback. Arianna Rehak is one of the association world's most enthusiastic originators and evangelists for the value of this new approach:

> *When you bring people together to solve a problem, the final result is so much more powerful than what any individual could accomplish. I got input from dozens and dozens of conversations. I could point to multiple design aspects that resulted from advice I received along the way. So, my philosophy of community development is certainly very bottom up.*

Value Talent

Talent and the environment that develops around it are, without doubt, among the highest priorities in innovative organizations. Entrepreneurs realize that their businesses can only be as good as the people they hire. For this group, employees are as valuable as their customers. Many have developed extensive vetting processes to ensure that they are putting people on the team who will perpetuate the right attitude and beliefs. Charlie Judy built a business around evaluating and improving organizational culture. A personal epiphany led Judy to study what makes cultures successful and how employees find fulfillment:

> *If I was missing a set of behaviors that fuel my fire, I don't care if the company has made every list of the best places to work in the world. It will not provide an environment in which I can be successful.*
>
> *Organizations need to achieve that level of clarity. You have to understand the characteristics of work in your culture. That specific information allows employers to hire people who are the right fit for their community, and it can help prospective employees avoid situations where they will not thrive.*

Kevin Hostutler is passionate about shaping a positive atmosphere in which innovation can flourish. Giving employees voice and recognition are a high priority, and he has developed several programs that are both interactive and fun to achieve those goals:

> *Recently, to get everyone thinking creatively, we added a Shark Tank component to our company meetings. It gives any employee with an idea a platform to present their innovation. The concepts can range from technology tools to work environment and process improvement, but the request must be specific. The goal is to get one or more executives to sponsor the initiative. We work with submitters on their pitches to help them consolidate their thoughts, articulate their proposition, and have the courage to defend their idea in front of the entire company.*

Transparency and openness are recommended by Tim Ward as antidotes for dysfunction and a means to keep ideas and enthusiasm flowing:

> *We strive for no drama and no ego. We encourage everyone to speak their mind and to identify what is not working. It's a good strategy for getting engagement and buy-in.*

Developing people is as important for Amith Nagarajan as expanding his business, and he sees one activity as a corollary of the other:

> *When you grow people, the by-product is that you grow your business. That's really where the fun is. Your purpose statement and core values become the foundational layers of culture. They provide an agreed-upon set of behaviors.*

Disappearing boundaries in the workplace was an ongoing theme. Geography is no longer an obstacle. Employers can cherry-pick talent from across the globe, on an as-needed basis. This ad hoc way of operating brings both efficiencies and challenges that have yet to be fully realized. But the availability of a broad base of expertise on demand is something that associations need to leverage. David Caruso, who has run a virtual business since 2005, observed that being freed from the barriers of location has improved his ability to find the right talent and changed his management style:

> *Today, we are able to hire the best people for the job, no matter where they live, and technology allows us to bring them together seamlessly. When you have the right team, you don't worry about distractions. I know that our employees don't need an office or a manager looking over their shoulder to be productive.*

Understand Your Customers

Although technology helps us work more effectively, in the digital age the role of technology moves beyond action and into the realm of understanding. Using data to develop a deep and empathetic perspective on members/customers is at the heart of digital transformation. Teri Carden explains how some of her association clients are using their data to address member needs:

> *We've seen several associations exporting data from their online communities and analyzing it with artificial intelligence tools to extract member sentiments and find fresh solutions to problems. Instead of playing a guessing game, they're allowing the members to drive the conversation. Doing more listening can also generate ideas for products and services.*

Adele Cehrs cautions that organizations need to move beyond viewing constituents as a group and begin treating them as individuals by offering customized services that speak to personal preference. Many other contributors echoed this theme, especially in regard to membership and how it is packaged and presented. Cehrs urges leaders to use technology to improve the public's ability to experience their brands on multiple levels:

> *For example, if I want a coffee at Starbucks, I can order it on my phone and pick it up without interacting with anyone. On the other hand, if I want to sit by the fake fireplace, have a chat with the barista, and hear some easy listening jazz, that's available too. I can relate to the brand on my own terms. Starbucks is not dictating my behavior. Hilton offers another take on this concept. If you are a rewards member you can check in and have access to your room on your phone and completely bypass the reception desk. In order to*

> *retain their privileged place in the market, associations must offer their members a similarly broad range of choices.*

Recognition that an association's customers can, and should, extend far beyond the limits of traditional membership was another common theme. Contributors identified many opportunities for associations to expand their circle of influence, particularly in the areas of education and certification.

Use Data to Drive Decisions

The fancy graphics and charts that technology makes available are not just show ponies. Statistics and analytics should form the basis for decision-making. Objective information can take the politics out of the dialogue and give leaders a stronger rationale for strategy and different approaches to planning. Design thinking, which Garth Jordan, used to help the Healthcare Financial Management Association develop its Netflix-like business model, is a problem-solving methodology that uses data to create action plans:

> *After multiple rounds of research and loops in the design process, our solution modeled on the successful Netflix formula emerged. You can access us on any platform—whether you are in your home office, on your phone at Starbucks, or searching your tablet during a meeting—it doesn't matter. Members can view one webinar, become certified, contribute to our online community, or utilize our entire experience portfolio for an all-inclusive price. We're also watching the statistics carefully to ensure that the content we roll out is relevant.*

See Broadly

For us, these interviews highlighted themes that are important for success in our consulting business as well as for our clients in the association community. The behaviors and attitudes that are outlined in the book overlap and intertwine. They are certainly more nuanced than we can explore in this brief summary. As a whole, these characteristics represent qualities that we believe are essential for associations and all other businesses to operate successfully in Association 4.0, or an evolving technological environment.

We've created the Association 4.0 Assessment to help our clients evaluate where they can incorporate new thinking, stimulate growth, and realign business models. The tool identifies strengths as an Association 4.0 organization as well as readiness for digital transformation in seventy-two areas across these nine domains:

- Strategy
- Decision Making
- Innovation
- People/Skills/Culture
- Processes/Operations
- Technology/Systems
- Metrics/Analytics
- Revenue
- Cybersecurity

To learn more about the Association 4.0 Assessment tool, please visit, https://www.orgsource.com/what-we-do/transformational-change-management/.

Be Brave

Becoming a transformer isn't for the fainthearted. It requires the courage to never stop being a pioneer, a student, and a risk-taker. It demands the humility to ask questions, to experiment, and to make mistakes and start over again. Finally, transformation requires seeing beyond the present to the potential. No one can execute all of this perfectly. Our contributors would tell you that perfection is far from the point. The joy is in the challenge. Solving problems and creating ideas, activities, and things that didn't exist before is the essence of the entrepreneurial spirit, and that spirit is the breath of innovation that fuels Association 4.0.

JOIN THE CONVERSATION

Typically, a book is a one-way conversation, but it doesn't have to be. During the interviews, many thought-provoking questions surfaced. Questioning is a powerful tool that can make impactful changes to you as a person and your organization. Below is a catalog of questions that will help you get the conversation started.

Culture

Could your organization benefit from channeling fear productively?

- What are some of the issues that cause fear among your members?
- How could those challenges be used to drive productive behavior?

Do you and your team take advantage of mentoring opportunities?

- Do you have methods to benchmark your skills/progress against other executives in the field?

Do you approach business questions with humility?

- Do you regularly seek broad-based advice and information?

- What external groups or people could provide valuable input in your decision-making processes?

Do you cultivate a shared sense of responsibility within your organization?

- What activities promote this concept?

Does your organization operate with a growth mindset?

- If you answered yes, what activities validate that response?
- If you answered no, what steps could you take to develop a more growth-oriented culture?

Has your organization adopted any characteristics of the open-source concept?

- Would becoming more collaborative be beneficial?
- If so, with whom could you collaborate or partner?

Have you defined workplace values?

- If so, are you living up to those standards?

How does your organization ensure that employees enjoy what they do?

- Is employee fulfillment a priority?
- Is that value conveyed throughout the workplace?

How does your organization manage risk?

- Are there strategies you could implement to become more risk-tolerant?

How does your organization work to cultivate diversity?

- Are you diverse demographically?
- Are you also diverse in style, personality and opinion?

- If not, what is holding you back?

How fluid is your organization's hierarchy?

- Do you seek ideas from all areas of the organization?

How is failure viewed in your organization?

- What would need to happen to make failure a more productive learning experience?
- Do you agree that failure is necessary for growth?

If you have virtual or temporary employees, what steps do you take to help them participate in your culture?

- Do employees at your organization have enough opportunities to coalesce as a team and to socialize?
- What additional experiences could you offer?

Is the upside-down pyramid the right organizational model for the future?

- On a scale of 1-10 how hierarchical is your organization?
- What are the benefits of an upside-down organizational chart?
- What are the drawbacks?

What behavior in your organization hinders progress?

- How could your organization change that behavior?

What behavior occurs in your organization that advances productivity and success?

What does authenticity mean to you?

- Is this a quality that is promoted in your organization?

What role does intellectual curiosity play in your organization?

- Are your teams encouraged to explore ideas for their own sake?
- Are questions welcomed, even when they might be disruptive?
- Do you hire people who love learning? How do you evaluate that quality during the interview process?

Would the Warrior Spirit be a good fit for your team?

- What does being a warrior in the workplace mean to you?

Data and Analytics

Are you using data to answer important questions?

- If not, what could you do to create a more data driven culture?

Is your organization using data effectively?

- Is your AMS an effective data collection platform?
- Are you missing important information?
- How could you collect that data?

Governance

Do you agree with the idea that people who are still striving to get to the top will be the most future oriented?

- How does that statement impact your organization?
- How could you identify board members who are future oriented?

Has fear of the board's disapproval kept you from making necessary changes?

- How could you manage that situation more effectively?

How diverse in thought, experience and demographics is your board?

- What issues are preventing greater diversity?

How well do your organization's board and staff communicate?

- Is dialogue conducted with trust and respect?
- Do both groups listen equally?
- What steps would create better understanding between the two groups?

What are some of the differences between how for-profit and nonprofits operate?

- Are there ways in which your organization operates like a for-profit?
- If so, would it be beneficial to expand those areas?
- How can associations operate more like businesses without compromising their values?

Human Resources

Are virtual teams in your organization's future?

- Have you studied how to manage and lead remote employees and teams?

Are you making an adequate investment in your management team's professional development?

- How is learning shared across the organization?

Do you agree with the idea that employees should come first?

- If yes, why?
- If no, why not?

- How high a priority are employees in your organization?
- Are the people in some positions valued more highly than others?

Do you and your team take advantage of mentoring opportunities?

- Do you have methods to benchmark your skills/progress against other executives in the field?

Do you have enough self-starters and innovators on your teams?

- How do you identify people with those qualities?

Do you have the right balance of soldiers to artisans on your teams?

- How do you keep the groups separate enough to allow each to do their job?
- Does information flow between the two groups?
- If not, how could you enhance communication?

Does your association have a strategy for attracting and retaining a new generation of employees?

- How have younger employees changed the way that your organization operates?

Does your organization give employees voice and purpose?

- If not, what could you be doing to provide a more meaningful experience for your team?

How are your teams building skills to use future technology?

- Are you able to launch experimental/learning projects?
- If not, what barriers need to be removed?

How does your hiring process vet for cultural fit?

- Are the behaviors and attitudes that contribute to your organization's positive culture clearly defined?
- How are staff educated about culture, behavior and attitude?

How does your organization ensure that employees enjoy what they do?

- Is employee fulfillment a priority?
- Is that value conveyed throughout the workplace?

How fluid is your organization's hierarchy?

- Do you seek ideas from all areas of the organization?

If you have virtual or temporary employees, what steps do you take to help them participate in your culture?

- Do employees at your organization have enough opportunities to coalesce as a team and to socialize?
- What additional experiences could you offer?

What does the idea of creating a work experience customized to the employee mean to you?

- Is this something that would be beneficial for your organization?

What role does freelance talent have to play in your organization?

- What are the pros and cons of using freelancers?
- What is the appropriate mix of full-time to freelance support?
- What cultural adjustments are needed to integrate freelancers into an organization?

Innovation

Are there gaps in service that your organization could fill?

- Do you have a process for identifying those new sources of revenue?

Could the concept of failing fast and failing small be helpful to your organization?

- How could this idea be implemented with your programs and services?

Do you agree that the CEO needs to be an innovator?

- Why or why not?

Does your organization have a formalized process for innovation?

- Would identifying specific brainstorming formats be helpful?

Does your organization operate with a growth mindset?

- If you answered yes, what activities validate that response?
- If you answered no, what steps could you take to develop a more growth-oriented culture?

Does your organization routinely scan the environment for future trends?

- What strategies do you employ?
- Who is charged with this responsibility and how do results get communicated?

How could an association "presell" products?

- What are some effective strategies for evaluating success before bringing a product to market?

How does your organization manage risk?

- Are there strategies you could implement to become more risk-tolerant?

What challenges in your organization could also offer the seeds for growth?

- Would a systematic approach to identifying those opportunities be beneficial?

What do you think about the National Association of REALTORS® project REALTOR® University?

- Are there gaps in the market that your association could fill?

What is the balance between innovation and process in your organization?

- Are you creating space for innovation?
- Are you offering structure for execution?

Who are the innovators and risk-takers on your staff?

- Do you provide the freedom for them to be creative?
- What departments could serve as incubators for new ideas?
- What does giving people the white space to be creative mean?

Who needs to be a visionary in your organization and why?

- Are you striking the right balance between big picture thinkers and doers?
- Are there visionaries in your organization who have yet to be identified?

Leadership

Are leaders born or made?

- Which is more important skill or character?
- What can be done to create more effective leaders?

Do you agree that courage is an important value for CEOs?

- What prevents CEOs from acting courageously?
- What could be done to eliminate those barriers?

Do you agree that the CEO needs to be an innovator?

- Why or why not?

Do you approach business questions with humility?

- Do you regularly seek broad-based advice and information?
- What external groups or people could provide valuable input in your decision-making processes?

Do you believe that success rests with picking the right leader? Why or why not.

- Can great teams survive poor leadership? Why or why not?
- What can an organization do to mitigate subpar leadership?

How important are productivity and sustainability in your decision-making process?

- How do you evaluate whether an activity will contribute to those qualities?

Is fear a factor in your decision-making process?

- If yes, how can you mitigate fear and make deliberations more objective?

What is the predominate management style in your organization—more hand's off or more hand's on?

- Is that working for you?
- If yes, why? If no, why not?

Management and Operations

Do you have a process for evaluating programs to determine whether they continue to be relevant?

Does your organization have a structure that creates traction?

- Where are you weak?
- Where are you strong?
- Do you need help?

How does your organization balance the variables of customer experience versus revenue?

Is design thinking a concept that could be valuable to your organization?

Is your organization operating at peak efficiency?

- If not, where is improvement needed?
- How could you begin to implement better approaches?

Marketing

Are you making assumptions about your association's status in the marketplace?

- If so, what ideas could you abandon?
- How could you improve market scanning?

Do you agree with Stevens that social media is a competitor?

- If you answered yes, why and how is it a threat?
- If you answered no, explain why not?

Do you make a practice of testing ideas in the marketplace?

- Do you act on that feedback?

Do you use your mission as a sales tool?

- Is your mission carried through your branding initiatives?

How could an association "presell" products?

- What are some effective strategies for evaluating success before bringing a product to market?

How could virtual and in-person events be combined for greater impact?

What are the pros and cons of online versus in-person interaction?

- What is the appropriate mix of online versus in-person events?

Membership

Are members taking a back seat to mission in your organization?

- How is your mission serving the membership?
- Are you offering lip service or authenticity?
- What is the evidence that your mission is being effectively executed?

Are your members/customers investing in your success?

- How could you leverage member loyalty to move the association forward?

Do you know enough about your members to offer customized education and products?

- If not, how could you begin to gather this information?

How could virtual and in-person events be combined for greater impact?

How do you assess members' satisfaction with their customer experience?

How empathetic is your planning process?

- What could be done to increase the customer focus?

Is your organization providing members with an intuitive interface to information and knowledge?

- How far are you from integrating voice-based response into your customer service activities?

What are the pros and cons of online versus in-person interaction?

- What is the appropriate mix of online versus in-person events?

Strategy

Are there opportunities for co-creation in your organization?

- Where could this technique be used?
- Would it be beneficial for your group?
- Do you see any drawbacks to this approach? If so, what are they?

Are there signs of disruption in your organization's industry?

- If yes, how could you change and strengthen your position?

Do organizations really need to change as frequently as Stevens says they do?

- Are there drawbacks to frequent change?
- Is your organization equipped to quickly pivot when needed?

Has your organization identified its core purpose?

- Are you setting narrow priorities and executing around that purpose?
- What steps could you take to discover where your greatest value as an organization lies?

How skillful is your organization at adapting to changing business realities?

- What has changed in your business environment that your association has yet to address?
- What are the consequences of inertia?
- If you believe you are adapting successfully, what are your strengths?
- If you are not successfully adapting, what is holding you back?

Is your organization in the habit of thinking boldly?

- If not, what could stimulate a more audacious approach to problem-solving?

Is your organization's business model still viable?

- If you answered yes, make the case.
- If you answered no, what are the next steps?

What does connecting the dots mean to you?

- Is there the potential for synergy in your environment that you are missing?

Technology

Do you agree with Stevens that social media is a competitor?

- If you answered yes, why and how is it a threat?
- If you answered no, explain why not?

How are your teams building skills to use future technology?

- Are you able to launch experimental/learning projects?
- If not, what barriers need to be removed?

Is technology debt holding your organization back?

- How up to date are your systems?
- If you are using old technology, what are you doing to address the problem?
- If you currently don't have the resources to purchase updates, how could you streamline your current systems?

Is your organization providing members with an intuitive interface to information and knowledge?

- How far are you from integrating a voice-based response into your customer service activities?

What kinds of online interaction are occurring in your association community?

- Have they been successful? How would you define success?
- How could you expand on those opportunities?

CONTRIBUTORS

We are honored and appreciative that the following entrepreneurs shared their ideas, journey, and wisdom with us on this project. We encourage you to continue the conversation with these unique, purpose-driven leaders.

Sherry Budziak, CEO and Founder, .orgSource

Chapter 1: To Grow a Business, Be Prepared to Grow Yourself

My work is my vocation, my passion, and the realization of a childhood dream. The association space is my playing field. It gives me the opportunity to exercise skills that come naturally, such as resolving complex problems, identifying challenges and opportunities, and launching new ventures. It's also where I've learned to approach the unknown with enthusiasm and to embrace being an innovator and an agent of change.

https://www.orgsource.com/
info@orgsource.com
847-275-1840

Teri Carden, Co-Founder, 100Reviews

Chapter 20: Creating Their Own Success

A self-proclaimed girl geek in normal girl's clothing, I've been an association professional for 10 years. With the support of mentors, colleagues, volunteer leaders, and bosses, I was able to test and implement new technologies such as online communities, develop eye-catching marketing campaigns, introduce new social media streams, and jump headfirst into the mobile world. Currently, I'm on my own doing consulting projects for Online Community Results (www.onlinecommunityresults.com), Collaborative Family Law Council of Florida, and others. My entrepreneurial spirit is also being tested with my newest endeavor, Review My AMS (https://reviewmyams.com). Away from the computer screen, I love to cook, exercise, wrestle with the kids, explore craft cocktail bars, visit the beach, and enjoy time with my family and friends.

https://www.100reviews.com/
850-491-1390

David Caruso, Co-Founder and President, HighRoad Solutions

Chapter 13: Getting to Wow

I have over 25 years of experience growing ideas from start-up to profitable multimillion-dollar organizations that offer document management, automated digital marketing, software, professional services, and actionable data analytics. My key areas of expertise are in sales growth, marketing, and operations of start-up to Fortune 500/5000 organizations. Much of my career has been dedicated to implementing enhanced communication solutions. My primary responsibilities include growing and strengthening HighRoad's overall position as a leading digital marketing solution provider for associations and nonprofits.

https://www.highroadsolutions.com/home
info@highroadsolutions.com
703.297.8888

Adele Cehrs, CEO and Founder, When + How Agency

Chapter 4: Business Wonder Woman

I am a sought-after communications expert who has spoken at the United Nations twice in the past year. I am also a recurring contributor to the *Wall Street Journal*, *Inc.* and *Forbes*, and have written for *Inc.* magazine. A pioneer in the science of timing for brands and corporate communicators, I believe what you say won't matter if you don't know when and how to say it. Many of my insights appear in my 2015 book, *SPIKE Your Brand ROI: How to Maximize Reputation and Get Results*. Dubbed a Business Wonder Woman by the *Washington Business Journal*, I have worked with clients as varied as Lockheed Martin, DuPont, American Society of Association Executives, and former Vice President Joe Biden. My agency, Epic, was reinvented to focus on the science of timing and rebranded as When + How.

https://whenandhowagency.com/
703-646-9196

Roy Chomko, CEO, Adage Technologies

Chapter 18: An Operating System for Invention

My passion for technology, building things, and helping people led me to start three technology firms in the past 20 years that service IT infrastructure, application development, and all things digital. My specialties include e-commerce, content management, web application development, cloud, and managed services. I continue to learn and grow every day in leading and managing technology organizations.

https://www.adagetech.com/
312-258-1200

Don Dea, FASAE, Co-Founder and Owner, Fusion Productions

Chapter 2: Connecting the Dots

I have authored several books published by the ASAE Foundation on the internet, digital transformation, and online education and have penned articles on technology, healthcare 2020, association leadership and digital transformation. I co-produce digitalNow, an executive summit for association/nonprofit leaders. I have served in senior executive roles in global technology, marketing, and real estate and have co-founded several high technology companies and a construction firm. I served as Special Assistant to the Attorney General, Department of Justice, in the President's Executive Exchange Program.

https://www.fusionproductions.com/
producer@fusionproductions.com
585-872-1900

Brent Gibson, MD, MPH, CAE, FACPM, CCHP-P, Managing Director, NCCHC Resources, Inc.

Chapter 19: Selling the Mission

In addition to being Chief Health Officer for the National Commission on Correctional Health Care as well as Managing Director, NCCHC Resources, Inc., the Commission's technical consulting affiliate, I am a Certified Association Executive with 8 years of experience in association leadership, 12 years of public health leadership experience, and 16 years of service as a licensed physician. As proven leaders in public health and correctional health care, our team at NCCHC Resources, Inc., is dedicated to identifying and supporting critical opportunities to improve quality in correctional health care.

https://www.ncchc.org/NCCHC-Resources
info@ncchcresources.org
773-880-1460

Kevin Hostutler, President, CEO and Co-founder, ACGI Software

Chapter 9: The Opportunistic Entrepreneur

With 25 years of experience working in the association management software industry, I provide strategic vision, planning, and overall leadership for ACGI Software. Since founding ACGI in 1996, I have focused on building an exceptional team of professionals and setting the direction for ACGI's product lines. I am also involved in managing relationships with customers, executive management leadership, and maintaining strategic alignment across all departments. Prior to ACGI, I was project manager for a leading association management software company for over 6 years. A native of Ohio, I graduated magna cum laude in Engineering Science from the Franciscan University of Steubenville.

https://www.acgisoftware.com
410-772-8950

Garth Jordan, MBA, CSM, CSPO, CDT, Chief Strategy Officer and Senior Vice President, Healthcare Financial Management Association

Chapter 15: Designing Differently

Over the past 15 years I have served in various executive roles and have been able to lead diverse teams through strategic planning and successful execution; build businesses with excellent customer-value propositions; and develop a well-rounded business and cultural acumen geared toward achieving an organization's goals through high-performing teams. Recently, after HFMA designed and executed a complete digital transformation of the business model, retention rates increased over 5 percent and new member acquisition increased over 20 percent.

https://www.hfma.org
gjordan@hfma.org
708-531-9600

Charlie Judy, Chief People Officer, Intelligent Medical Objects

Chapter 12: To Get Where You Want to Go, Know Who You Are

For two decades I was a human resources executive with some of the world's most prominent professional services organizations. Perhaps because of my penchant for disrupting management norms, I was reputed to be a future-of-work pundit with an enthusiasm for workplace culture. Meaningful work is about intentionally and simply engineering workplace cultures to fuel a more purposeful career experience and to accelerate enterprise growth. We are doing that at Intelligent Medical Objects (www.imohealth.com), a world-class healthcare technology company. In 2015 I founded WorkXO®, a preeminent cloud-based workplace culture assessment and analytics software, which was purchased in 2018 by QuestionPro. Much of what I share in this book is based on spending the following year and a half integrating our product with their platform while also building out a larger suite of workforce analytics solutions.

https://www.linkedin.com/in/charliejudy

Tracy King, MA, CAE, CEO and Chief Learning Strategist, InspirEd

Chapter 8: Making Butterflies—The Power of Transformational Learning

I specialize in the transformation of organizations, leaders, and learners, and I advance workforces by consulting with organizations on the business of learning and program design. I also coach executives on implementing innovations while navigating the competitive continuing education (CE) landscape. I offer my own e-learning courses, training workshops, and transformational leadership retreats to advance the profession. I am the award-winning author of *Competitive Advantage: Create Continuing Education That Is Profitable, Sustainable, and Impactful* as well as a thought leader, skilled facilitator, invited speaker, and DELP scholar. My work has been featured in hundreds of nationally syndicated television, newspaper, and magazine outlets.

https://www.inspired-ed.com/

Joseph (Joey) Knecht, CEO, Managing Director, Proteus.co

Chapter 11: Leveraging Opportunity From Inspiration to ROI

Growing up in the New Y metro area, I learned the science of navigating through challenges by helping engage diverse groups of people to find solutions at an early age. From my early years of leading street-ball leagues with peers in my Long Island neighborhood to a host of other entrepreneurial pursuits as a young man, this talent to identify the needs of customers and engage them in solutions shaped the contribution I now extend to international business-to-business (B2B) leaders across all industries. Today as CEO of Midwest-based Proteus.co, my focus is on leveraging technology to empower and engage buyers in complex B2B sales cycles.

https://www.proteus.co
402-420-5024

Hugh Lee, President, Fusion Productions

Chapter 2: Connecting the Dots

I am President of Fusion Productions, a 40+ year old Rochester, New York, based company that integrates digital media production, meeting & event design, and e-learning services. My industry involvements and accomplishments include being a board member of the American Society of Association Executives, Meeting Professionals International, and the New York Society of Association Executives. I am the founder of digitalNow, a nationally recognized summit for CEOs of non-profit organizations focusing on leading in the digital age. And author of over 35 books, publications and articles.

https://www.fusionproductions.com/
producer@fusionproductions.com
585-872-1900

Sandy Marsico, Founder and CEO, Sandstorm Design

Chapter 5: Confidence and Books Grow a Company

At age 24 I founded a boutique agency that thrived on exceptional and strategic work, with high energy in an environment in which there's always room for growth and change. Now I lead an incredible, passionate, and dynamic team and counsel CEOs on culture as a growth and brand strategy. Sandstorm has been featured on CNBC and been listed among Chicago's 101 Best & Brightest Companies to Work For. Sandstorm has grown into Chicago's leading brand experience agency for organizations that include Crown (NYSE CCK), National Association of REALTORS, Blue Cross Blue Shield, Campbell's, Rotary, and Discovery Education. Having conducted over 3,000 in-depth interviews and usability studies, we have mastered the art of uncovering insights to elevate brand experiences.

https://www.sandstormdesign.com/
773-348-4200

Ben Martin, CAE, Executive Director, The Review Society and Chief Engagement Officer, Online Community Results

Chapter 20: Creating Their Own Success

I help organizations realize return on investment in online communities. My clients include the Institute of Electrical and Electronics Engineers, AAAS, Specialty Food Association, American Business Women's Association, American Association for Clinical Chemistry, and American Medical Informatics Association.

http://reviewsociety.org
https://www.onlinecommunityresults.com/

Amith Nagarajan, Executive Chairman, rasa.io

Chapter 14: Driven by Purpose

I help brands engage with their customers, prospects, and partners via Smart Newsletters - delivered automatically through email.

https://rasa.io/

Kevin Ordonez, Co-Founder, .orgCompanies

Chapter 1: To Grow a Business, Be Prepared to Grow Yourself

I am a passionate innovator, life-long entrepreneur, speaker, and author. I help associations build value, innovate within and discover strategy. I am a self-proclaimed problem finder. I bring an unprecedented level of commitment to my consulting clients at .orgSource and to the association leaders in .orgCommunity.

https://orgcompanies.com/

findus@orgcommunity.com

630-697-5141

Joanna Pineda, Founder, CEO, and Chief Troublemaker, Matrix Group International, Inc.

Chapter 7: Going Deep—A Commitment to Solving the Right Problem

I am CEO and Chief Troublemaker at Matrix Group International, Inc., a web design and development firm based in Arlington, Virginia, that helps trade associations, professional societies, foundations, private firms, and think tanks do business online. I want to work with organizations that have big dreams, have senior leadership support for their online initiatives, aren't too dysfunctional and full of silos, and are looking for a partner to help them find their path online.

https://www.matrixgroup.net/
703-838-9777

Arianna Rehak, Co-founder and CEO, MatchBox Virtual Media

Chapter 6: Where Limitless Ideas Grow

When I was 7-years-old I lugged my toys and art supplies onto my front lawn with a sign bearing the title of my new venture: Rent-It. For a small price, my neighbors could rent out anything from a fairy stencil to a red marker. I made $1.15 in one day's work, but I attribute that to bad price pointing! From that day on, my entrepreneurial rigor only got stronger, but more significantly, it became more pointed.

I am a student of human nature, which has guided both my channels of learning and my career direction. I have learned that good intentions are not enough to get things done, and it is my ultimate goal to use both critical and creative thinking to achieve maximum impact.

Kim Robinson, CAE, President, FrontlineCo

Chapter 10: Strike the Balance: Seek Perfection, Inspire Vision

I serve as president of FrontlineCo. Previously, as the executive director of the Illinois Capital Development Board, I spent 4 years directing the state's $3 billion capital program. I am also a Certified Association Executive. I invite you to contact me for a strategic session regarding your association and where you'd like to take it.

https://frontlineco.com/
kim@frontlineco.com
217-528-3434

Dan Stevens, President, WorkerBee.TV

Chapter 17: A Passion to Be Unique

I am the President of WorkerBee.TV and enjoy helping associations improve their value and relevancy by leveraging the power of video and multimedia to improve their micro-marketing, micro-learning and credentialing and continued education capabilities.

https://workerbee.tv/

Sigmund VanDamme, Membership Software Evangelist, Community Brands

Chapter 3: Driven by the Creative Itch

I am an executive representative for the Community Brands portfolio of industry-leading membership software products and services. Part of my role is to deliver thought leadership through public speaking, webinars, white papers, and trade shows. In addition, I focus on customer advocacy through direct participation in product councils, advisory groups, and user communities.

https://www.communitybrands.com/

Meg Ward, Co-Founder, Gravitate Solutions

Chapter 16: Pursuing the Freedom to Shape their Future

I am an experienced executive skilled in strategic planning, business development, marketing strategy, and business operations. And I am a strong entrepreneurship professional who earned a BA from the University of Colorado at Boulder.

https://gravitatesolutions.com/
info@gravitatesolutions.com
703-579-6930

Tim Ward, Co-Founder and CEO, Gravitate Solutions

Chapter 16: Pursuing the Freedom to Shape their Future

I am an accomplished executive, technologist, entrepreneur, software engineer, systems architect, and consultant who is experienced in the start-up and profitable growth of innovative companies. I am an expert in the design, development, and maintenance of commercial software products and large distributed systems. I have strong interpersonal skills and a steadfast commitment to ethics and integrity.

https://gravitatesolutions.com/
info@gravitatesolutions.com
703-579-6930

ABOUT THE AUTHORS

Sherry Budziak
Founder, .orgSource and Co-Founder .orgCompanies

Most people who work for an association don't set out to have a career in the industry. My story is different. Ever since I was 14 years old, I wanted to work for a nonprofit. I discovered early how exciting it is to make a difference, and that thrill continues to inspire my personal and professional life.

At Valparaiso University, I was involved in AIDS awareness, date rape education, BACCHUS, Christmas in July, and many more philanthropic programs. My goal was to someday become an executive director and make a real impact in my community. At the time, a degree in nonprofit management was not offered, so I double majored in communications and political science.

The American Association of Neurological Surgeons/Congress of Neurological Surgeons (AANS/CNS) gave me my first chance to begin learning the ropes. David Martin, the assistant executive director at the time (now CEO at the Society of Critical Care Medicine), asked if I would help him create a website. In 1994, the internet was still largely uncharted territory, and we didn't have many examples to rely upon or inspire us. Although we took a lot of risks, in the end, we built an incredible online presence for the organization, which may have been one of the first association websites.

My experience with this new technology attracted interest from others. I was approached by the American Academy of Dermatology (AAD) to develop a for-profit subsidiary to help associations launch their online presence. It was an exciting and sometimes a scary challenge. My technology team and I survived the uncertainty of Y2K. We dealt with overheating server rooms and a host of other electronic nightmares.

Starting a business and selling to the association industry was a great adventure! As I advanced in the organization, I was once again asked to shoulder responsibilities for which I had no background. The executive director at the time, Tom Conway, CAE (now Chief Financial Officer at the American Association of Clinical Endocrinologists), appointed me to take on what had become his "IT [information technology] headache." While it was more like a migraine, it gave me the experience I needed to start my consulting practice.

My career began with two association executives who took a chance on a young woman with more ambition than experience and the courage to try new things and take risks. The thrill of entrepreneurship—developing new products and revenue streams—led me to start a consultancy. For the last twenty-five years, .orgSource has supported associations with a wide range of services, including strategic planning, technology, marketing, and communications. Every day, I experience the value of my involvement with many organizations, their cultures, and their management. My career has been an incredible journey. I am thankful to those from whom I have learned along the way. I look forward to helping others grow, lead, and advance their missions!

Kevin Ordonez
Co-Founder, .orgCompanies

For as long as I can remember, I wanted to be a software and technology entrepreneur. Over the past twenty-five years, I have had my share of challenges and success. With .orgCommunity, I am now on company number six.

During college, I joined the Association for Computing Machinery (ACM). There, I discovered firsthand the value of learning from peers, networking, and a feeling of belonging. At the ACM conferences, I met technological giants—people like Steve Jobs and Bill Gates.

After graduating from college with degrees in computer science and mathematics, I was fortunate to work for a consulting company in the Washington, D.C., area run by very a successful entrepreneur. My clients were among the most powerful trade associations in the country. I quickly noticed that adopting and leveraging technology was a common struggle. A few years later, I was hired by an association to help manage their technology infrastructure. As an "insider," I witnessed firsthand how far this organization was behind the curve. I realized that many other groups were also using outdated infrastructure, manual workarounds, and systems to track constituents, and experiencing an absence of innovation.

This was a big opportunity for an entrepreneur! I was inspired to start my first software company aimed at providing associations with better tools to manage their members, prospects, and operations. Since then, I've had the ride of my life. I grew the company from three people with three computers in a basement to hundreds of staff in multiple locations around the country servicing thousands of organizations.

Even as a busy entrepreneur, I volunteered as much as my time allowed to the association industry. Over the last twenty years I have served on various committees and working groups as well as in leadership positions and on boards.

Experience has taught me that the most effective associations think like entrepreneurs and execute like Fortune 100 companies. There are several familiar mantras that reflect that concept. Here are a few of my favorites:

- What is your secret sauce? What do you offer that is uniquely yours?
- Get out of your comfort zone. Release creativity and innovation and welcome healthy debate.
- What is your TAM (total addressable market)? Think beyond "members."
- Be unique. Focus on your business, not your competition.
- A prospect is a prospect until they buy or die. Never give up on your prospects.
- Everyone is in sales. You, your volunteers, your staff, and even your detractors are out there selling for you (or against you).

The right leadership can transform an association, jump-start its mission, and create boundless opportunities. As Steve Jobs famously said, "The people who are crazy enough to think that they can change the world, are the ones who do."

ALSO AVAILABLE

Association 4.0™: Positioning for Success in an Era of Disruption

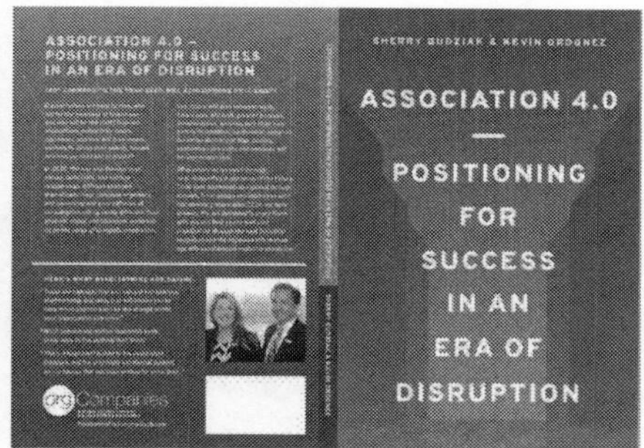

Available on Amazon.com

If you've been hiding from the future, get ready for a reality check. The Fourth Industrial Revolution is real. It's here. It's now. Let the experts guide you toward making the leap to Association 4.0™. This book is mandatory reading for association professionals.

Twenty-three association leaders who are innovators and cultural shape-shifters share their experiences with disruption.

Made in the USA
Monee, IL
11 February 2020